LANDS OF THE
HIMALAYAS

FLINT RIVER

LANDS

HIMA

Text by DENNIS GUNTON

OF THE
LAYAS

Photographs by JANEZ SKOK

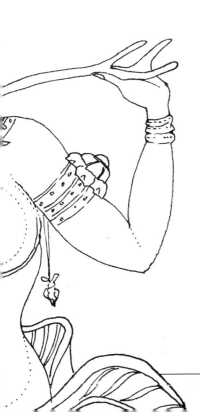

A Motovun Group Book
© Flint River Press Ltd 1995

First published in the U.K. by
FLINT RIVER PRESS Ltd
28 Denmark Street
London WC2H 8NJ

ISBN: 1 871489 13 X

Originated and developed by
Bato Tomasevic

Design:
Gane Aleksic

Editor:
Madge Phillips

Captions:
Janez and Ines Skok

Drawings by
Milica Bacic-Mujbegovic

Additional photographs (nos 211-229):
Robert Harding Picture Library, London

Typeset by Avalon, London

Organisation by Eurocity Associates, London

Colour separation by Delo, Ljubljana

Printed and bound by
Tiskarna Ljudska Pravica, Ljubljana

CONTENTS

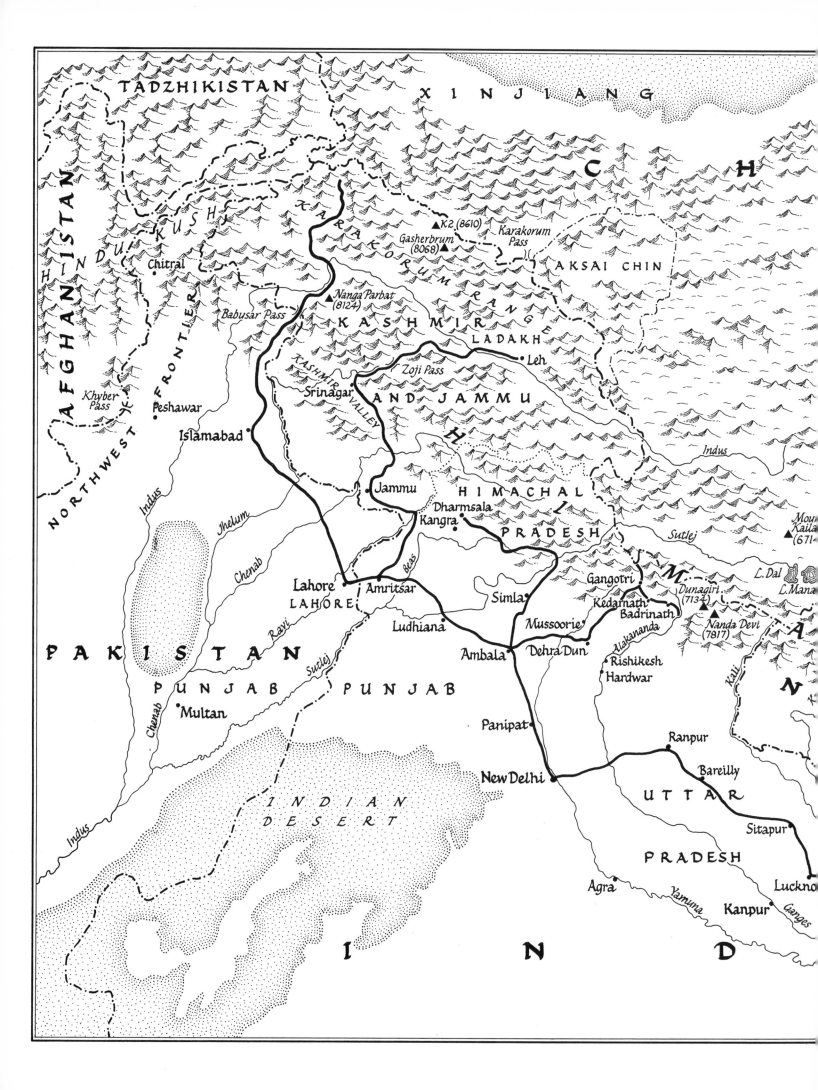

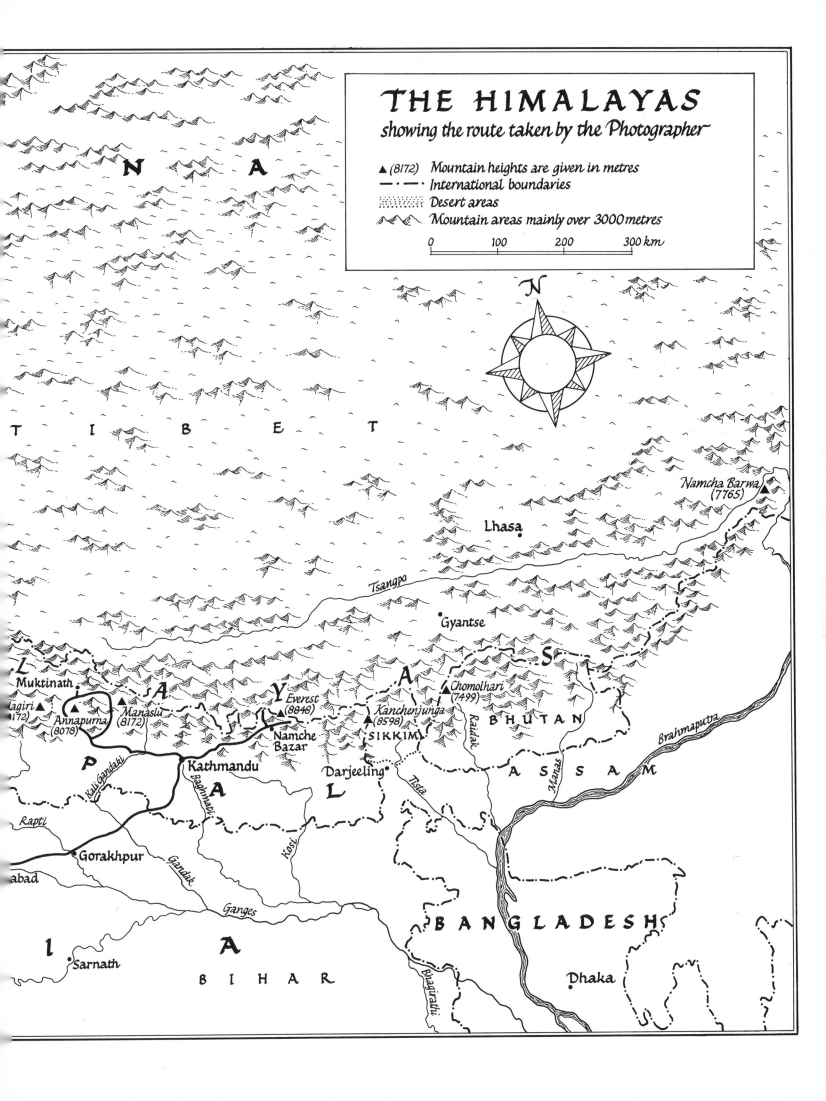

'SOME HIDDEN MOUNTAINS'

'From time to time God causes men to be born—and thou art one of them—who have a lust to go abroad at the risk of their lives and discover news—today it may be of a far-off thing, tomorrow of some hidden mountains...'

Kim
Rudyard Kipling (1865-1936)

Almost as enduring as the Himalayas are the two questions: How do you pronounce the word? Where are the boundaries? Most people say Hima*layas* with the accent on the third syllable, though Him-*ah*-layas comes closer to the pronunciation of those who live there. Some prefer the singular form, Himalaya, but the plural version is being increasingly used and has been adopted here.

Defining the geographical boundaries immediately raises issues regarding foothills and when they become mountains. And whilst most agree the vast mountain belt stretches from Nanga Parbat in the west to the Namcha Barwa in the east—both peaks are over 25,000 ft (7,813 m.) and stand 1,550 miles (2,480 km) apart—it is a symmetrical demarcation which excludes the Hindu Kush and Karakorum. Such symmetry has its uses, but does not clearly define the limits of a great mountain system. Rather more rewarding is to leave aside precise definitions and to take instead the mountains where they are to be found, delighting in the enduring magic which envelopes our planet's supreme workshop of primeval energy.

No area on the earth's surface has more evidently moulded character than the Himalayas, a region where the physical and measurable coalesce with the timeless and spiritual. Climbing Everest typifies the one, worshipping the heritage of Hindu gods the other. Either way the Himalayas embody man's eternal struggle towards self-assertion and self-knowledge, whether through an ascent of the all too awesomely visible or a study of the misty origins of mankind.

Foreign influences have made their mark on, but left intact, the legendary Himalayas, a word derived from the Sanskrit *hima* and *alaya*, meaning 'abode of snows'. A vast mountain system stretching 1,500 miles (2,400 km.) and sweeping along the borders of Afghanistan, Pakistan, India, Nepal, Sikkim, Bhutan and China, the region's fascination rests on its jagged peaks, massive glaciers, turbulent rivers, wildwood valleys and the chilling loneliness that undoubtedly inspires the respectful spiritual attitude of those who dwell there.

Relief. Covering an area of 229,500 square miles (594,400 sq. km.) roughly the size of France, the Himalayas are the most dominant section of the mountains that extend uninterrupted halfway around the world from northern Africa to the east coast of Asia. Edged on the north-western

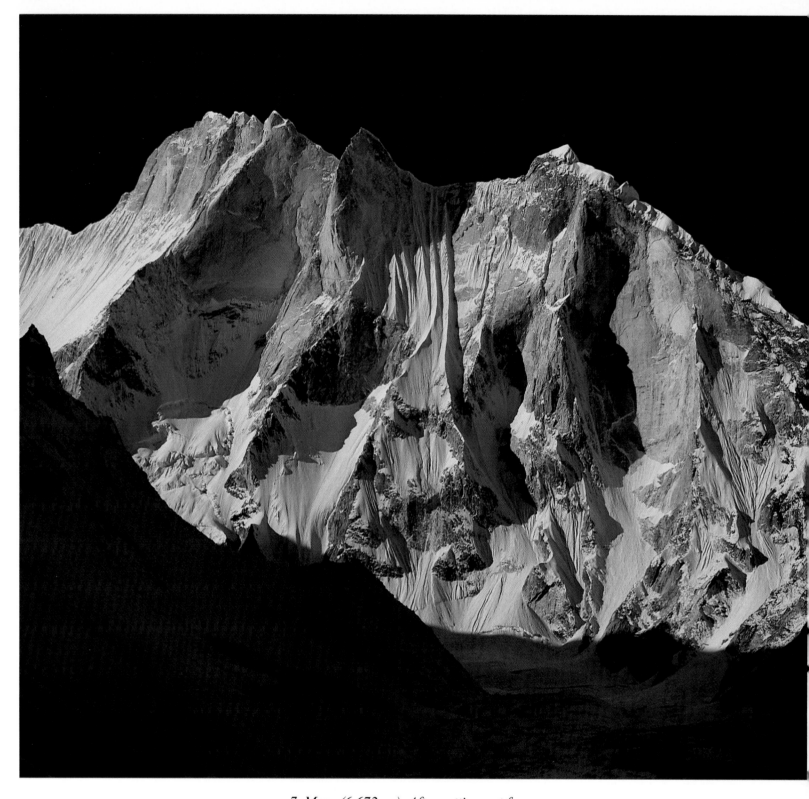

7. Meru (6,672 m.). After setting out from Tapovan and ascending the moraine wall at the foot of the west ridge of Shivling, one of the most beautiful mountains of the Garhwal region comes into view. The glittering granite wall of Meru, the subtle lines that shape its east face exert a strange fascination.

8. Bhagirathi II (6,512 m.) and III (6,454 m.), two peaks of the Bhagirathi group that dominates the Nanadavan plateau and the Gangotri Glacier above Gaumukh, the source of the Bhagirathi River that further downstream becomes the Ganges.

9. Thamserku (6,623 m.). Seen from the ridge that surrounds Namche Bazar and looking towards the south-east, the mountain appears so forbiddingly steep it is no wonder it was conquered only in 1963, by British climbers.

10. Ama Dablam (6,856 m.), literally 'Mother's Necklace', also known as the Giant's Tooth, occupies a dominating position above the River Imja Khola in the Solo-Khumbu region. The first ascent was by a New Zealand expedition in 1961.

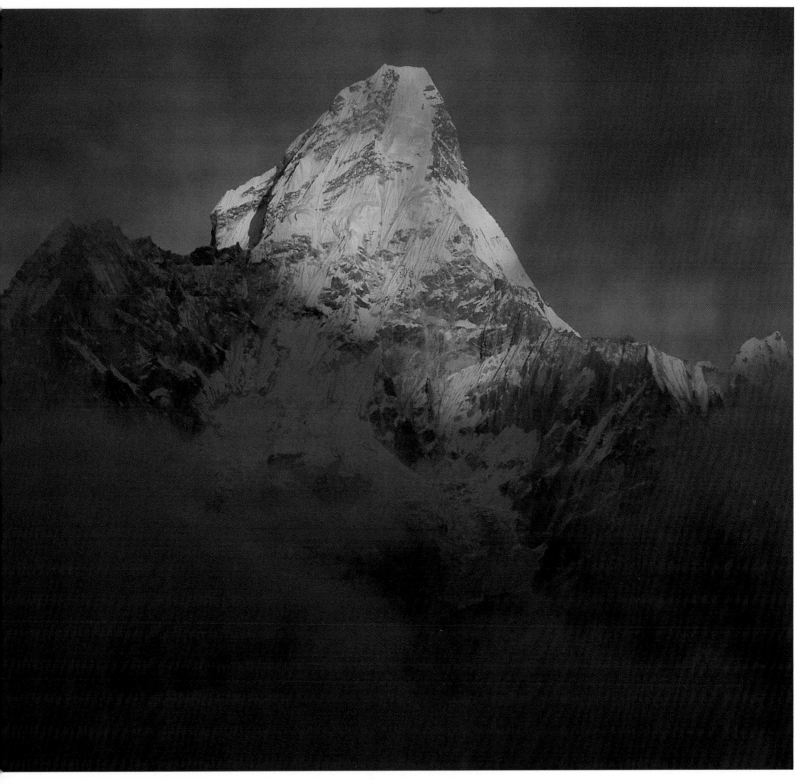

11. Lhotse (8,516 m.), in the vast Khumbu Himal range. Its name (from 'lho' = south and 'tse' = peak) in fact means peak south of Mount Everest, which is just discernible peeping over the Nuptse ridge. Fourth highest in the world, Lhotse was first climbed in 1956 by a Swiss team. (p. 22, top)

12-14. Mount Everest (8,848 m.), part of the immense Khumbu Himal, lies on the Nepalese-Chinese border. After ten previous attempts by British teams, it was finally scaled on May 29, 1953 by Edmund Hillary, a New Zealander, and Sherpa Tensing Norgay from India. (pp.22-23)

side by the mountain ranges of the Hindu Kush and the Karakorums, on the east by the kingdoms of Bhutan, Sikkim and Nepal, the Himalayas vary between 125 and 250 miles in width, rather like a quarter-moon with a concave entry upon the high plateau of Tibet, which itself has an average elevation of 10,000 ft (3,250 m.). Across the widest section are the most prominent peaks, which jut above the snow line, towering over the vast snow fields that nourish the growth of huge glaciers and furnish the fountain-heads of the narrow, turbulent Himalayan rivers. On the fringes of the mountains, constituting the greater part and enjoying seasons free of snow and ice, are the foothills, where farming is possible. Tea-growing is a major industry in India and hill stations such as Mussoorie (6,576 ft, 2,005 m.) are as refreshing today as they were when established by the civil servants of the British raj escaping the relentless summer heat of the plains more than a century ago. Whilst the romance of the Himalayas may be embodied in their soaring peaks and high passes, the tangible beauty is found in the valleys lodged at their roots.

Much as those peaks may look as if they were cast as the earth first cooled, in geological terms they are of remarkably recent origin. One hundred million years ago, India was separated from Asia by the Sea of Tethys; perhaps eighty million years ago the pre-Cambrian rock (created by heat and pressure as the earth cooled) forming a frontier of what is now India, thrust against the much softer marine sediment coastline of what is now Tibet. As India pushed against the Asian landmass to the north, so the Himalayas were thrust upwards and the Sea of Tethys was shouldered aside. In as little as the last one and a half million years, the mountains have risen 4,500 ft (1,500 m.) or as high as the highest point in the British Isles. This fantastic interplay of hard rock and layers of what had been a soft seabed became topped by ice and snow to create a rolling panorama which has inspired poetry, cradled religions and encouraged man to search for something within himself as exalted as the summits he can see.

Few will deny that the sight of the Himalayas is one of the most exciting and spiritually uplifting experiences. Only businessmen flying on the very early Indian Airlines Airbus from Delhi to Calcutta seem to remain impervious. I always asked for a 'port outer, starboard home' seat at the window and was invariably taken to task by fellow-passengers who pulled down their blinds to be able to sleep, and asked exceptions, such as myself, to do likewise, in the righteous tone usually adopted towards smokers or those unable to get their seat in the upright position. But this is only a contemporary phenomenon among frequent fliers; the Himalayas have always exerted a profound influence upon the plains-dwellers. And because, in the days before aviation, the latter's technology prohibited any easy physical incursion, the mountains, through pilgrimage, became a way to holiness via holy places.

From the 24,000-ft (7,500 m.) heights of the Hindu Kush in the west to Namcha Barwa, 25,445 ft (7,765 m.) in the east, the great range rises highest in Nepal, where there are nine of the fourteen highest peaks in the world: Dhaulagiri 26,810 ft (8,172 m.), Annapurna 26,504 ft (8,078 m.), Manaslu 26,760 ft (8,156 m.), Cho Oyo 26,750 ft (8,153 m.), Gyachung Kang 15,991 ft (7,922 m.), Everest 29,028 ft (8,848 m.), Lhotse 27,923 ft (8,511 m.), Makalu 27,824 ft (8,481 m.) and Kanchenjunga 28,208 ft (8,598 m.). All the high peaks are permanently snow-capped, the snow-

5. Cho Oyu (8,153 m.), seen when approaching Gokyo from the direction of Namche Bazar. On the other side of the mountain lies Tibet. The peak was first scaled in 1954 by two Austrians and two Sherpas.

line varying between 14,760 ft (4,500 m.) and 18,700 ft (5,700 m.).

Climate. For there to be snow there has to be moisture-laden movements in the air. Two factors combine to determine the meteorological conditions along the mountain chain: the phenomenal height of the range and the impact of the summer monsoon along the southern slopes. Warm air rises above the heated land mass of India, drawing moisture from the Bay of Bengal and Arabian Sea, but since this cannot cross the Himalayas, there is precipitation all along the Indian side of the mountains, leaving very little for the arid Tibetan wastes to the north. On the whole, the eastern Himalayas, being nearer the equator than the western, tend to be warmer and attract more rain. Normally the rains begin to peter out in September, when the best weather settles in until December.

In the Himalayan region many factors influence climate: altitude, exposure to wind, proximity to glaciers... A place like Leh, in the Indus Valley, which annually receives only three to six inches of rain, experiences three months in winter with an average temperature of minus 10 degrees C. Yet in summer, in some places it is possible above 10,000 ft (3,000 m.) to dress in slacks and a short-sleeved shirt until the sun sets.

Rivers. Rainfall and melting snow along with hard rock combine to make turbulent cataracts of the Himalayan river system. About nineteen major rivers drain the mountains, the two biggest being the Indus and the Brahmaputra. Five of the remaining seventeen are associated with the Indus: the Jhelum, Chenab, Ravi, Beas and Sutlej; three others, the Tista, Raidak and Manas, are tributaries of the Brahmaputra. The remaining nine belong to the Ganges system: the Ganges itself and the Yamuna, Ramganga, Kali, Karnali, Rapti, Gandak, Baghmati and Kosi. It might be expected that the rivers from the world's highest watershed would fall about equally to the north and the south. In fact, only one, the Brahmaputra, drains to the north and flows 900 miles eastward before cleaving its way through north-east Assam and Bangladesh to discharge into the Bay of Bengal. Fast flows of brown, sedimented water running through deep gorges characterise the Himalayan river system, which in its upper reaches is excellently suited to power generation.

Vegetation. In Europe or North America, vegetation may vary very little over an 800-mile drive in a north-south line. In the Himalayas, where the classification can run from monsoon tropical through sub-tropical and temperate to the arctic, change comes more quickly and results from altitude rather than horizontal distances. Sir Joseph Dalton Hooker (1817-1911), son of the distinguished botanist who founded London's Kew Gardens, travelled to India in 1848 and spent two years classifying plant life. He began in the swamp areas near the Brahmaputra and noted, as do all visitors to the jungle, the variety of flora, the scarcity of fauna and that the place was overrun by insects.

Very roughly, vegetation relates to altitude like this:

Grasses, shrubs	to 16,000 ft (5,000 m.)
Conifers	to 11,500 ft (3,600 m.)
Oaks	to 9,000 ft (2,800 m.)
Laurels, schima, holly	to 5,900 ft (1,800 m.)
Rain forest	to 3,200 ft (1,000 m.)

Plant life will survive up to about 20,000 ft (6,100 m.).

Krishna, legendary Indian hero and ruler, who according to Indian tradition was the eighth incarnation of the deity Vishnu. His youthful adventures are recounted in the 'Mahabharata'.

Sir Joseph Hooker climbed to a height of 17,000 ft in pursuit of the 4,000 items he meticulously collected, classified and described in the staggering seven volumes of his *Flora of British India*. One genus that attracted Hooker's attention was the rhododendron, a tough plant capable of surviving in the cold conditions that prevail at altitudes of up to 12,000 ft (3,700 m.). In Nepal specimens can grow to 60 ft with a trunk measuring four feet in diameter. Altitude determines colour: the vivid red blossoms lower down give way to pink and white flowers at higher elevations. Hooker believed the small (two-inch) species grows higher up than any other shrub. By attracting insects, which in turn attract birds, the rhododendron is a major contributor to the maintenance of high-altitude ecosystems. Those overlaying the hillsides around Simla from March to May create as breathtaking a wild garden as one could hope to see.

From the general bleakness of the barren plateau at the western end of the Himalayas, movement eastwards to the alluvial soils of Kashmir sees more luxuriant vegetation, as well as extensive terracing to reduce the erosion caused by the monsoon. In the Darjeeling Hills the soil has a high humus content, coupled with an annual rainfall of 120 inches (300 cm.), making the hot-weather resort of Darjeeling at 7,000 ft (2,180 m.) the centre of perhaps the finest tea-growing area on earth.

Animal life. One unexpected consequence of the Gulf War of 1991 was the fall of thick layers of soot on the snow-covered slopes of Kashmir. The contamination came from the clouds of pollution, towering 15,000 ft, discharged from burning oil wells 2,000 miles away in Kuwait. Despite their rugged remoteness, the mountains and the wildlife they support are surprisingly vulnerable, most especially to the activities of mankind close at hand. All the more commendable, therefore, has been the fairly generous allocation of space, particularly in Bhutan, Nepal and India, for wildlife sanctuaries. Animals in the Himalayas have much to contend with. The Indian rhinoceros, for example, once common in the foothills, is becoming extinct. Leopards, too, are diminishing in numbers, not surprisingly given the value of their pelts and the fact, as an unattractive, chuckling furrier in Srinagar once told me, 'They do not have the sense to keep within boundaries of countries which are adopting Wildlife Preservation Acts.'

Ironically enough, the oldest wildlife sanctuary in India was founded by Edward James Corbett, author of the best-seller *Man-eaters of Kumaon*, who lived and hunted in the hills until, in 1935, he established the national park named after him. It has to be said that a visitor to a major zoo in Europe or North America is more likely to get a good view of Himalayan fauna than anyone trekking in their natural habitat. The chances of this are somewhat better in the game parks, which also offer the opportunity to learn more about the wildlife from wardens committed to its preservation.

Monkey, bear, wolf, leopard, tiger, deer, squirrel, jackal and ibex all make their home in the mountains, as does a rich variety of birds, including crows, kites, vultures, cuckoos, cranes, swallows, martins and egrets. Some birds have been seen above 18,000 ft (5,500 m.). Even higher, at 20,000 ft (6,100 m.), can be found the highest-living mammal, the collared pika, a member of the hare family. Above them, and beyond the tree line, only insects and spiders manage to survive the extreme temperature and the starved eco-system of the high Himalayas.

Fish are not generally found above 12,000 ft (3,700 m.): the water is too cold and the winter too long. During the summer monsoon period, rivers are turbulent and unless fish can adhere to boulders, they are swept downstream. However, in some lakes that warm easily, so encouraging aquatic vegetation, fish can live and breed. By contrast, deep, clear-water lakes fed by melted glaciers are not productive.

The wild yak is rarely seen, but there are plenty of the domesticated variety, which I once heard referred to as 'the four-legged-drive Himalayan answer to the Land Rover'. These splendid beasts of burden also provide milk, meat, wool and leather. Even when rancid, the butter made from yak milk is precious for burning in lamps in homes and monasteries. Muscle power, much of it human, visibly impels most activity in the Himalayas. In the animal kingdom the yak is, uniquely, hardy and docile enough to withstand the rigours of life at such an altitude.

Snakes are not often encountered, although about seventy species are found in Nepal alone; it is estimated that the ratio of sightings of poisonous to non-poisonous snakes is about one to ten. Once, staying with friends in Kathmandu, my wife asked the hostess why she kept so many geese. She replied that, shortly after moving into the house, they had discovered that a family of pit-vipers—definitely poisonous—had colonised the premises whilst they were vacant. After the vipers had been hunted and removed, geese were introduced to discourage any reptilian notions about reasserting squatters' rights. This reply did wonders for my wife's speed of reaction to any scuffling she heard, but nothing to help her sleep that night.

The veil of mystery and myth which has for so long swathed the high Himalayas is relentlessly being raised, but not all their secrets have been revealed. In 1933 the Tibetan Government forbade the overflying of the northern slopes of Mount Everest by the Houston Flying Expedition on the grounds that ferocious demons lived there and they should on no account be disturbed. The legendary yeti continues to fascinate and tantalise with reports of sightings, footprints (photographed in 1951 by Eric Shipton, one of the greatest mountaineers to climb the Himalayas), inhuman yells, piercing whistles, scalps (three exist in monasteries), fur (some found by Hillary was subsequently identified as belonging to a bear), and the Nepalese Government's insistence that no harm befalls any captured specimen (whilst offering Yeti service on Royal Nepal Airlines). There are one or two strands which are factual enough to keep the old yarn of the Abominable Snowman alive. Although the mountains have eternally been host to the supernatural, western accounts of the prehensile-limbed wanderer begin only at the turn of this century. Alleged sightings and even expeditions for the sole purpose of identifying the beast have continued down the years, but the only convincing evidence of its existence to date is the Shipton photograph comparing a climbing boot with an oval-shaped footprint, on which the big toe is shorter and stubbier than the others. When the photograph was taken, Shipton was climbing the Melungtse Glacier with a Sherpa companion. In the minds of the Sherpas, in particular, there is a strong conviction that some strange creature dwells in remote reaches of their homeland: Nepal's most famous inhabitant is its most elusive.

PEOPLES AND FAITHS

'He who goes to the Hills goes to his mother.'
Hindu saying

The Mountain Dwellers

To the outsider there frequently appears to be more by way of common denominators than there are distinctions among the Himalayan peoples. There are similarities in height, build, flat features, skin colour, hair, and in their deeply religious feelings. All the same, the separate identities are there, not surprisingly given the waves of immigration into the mountains from all points of the compass and the jostling for the most comfortable areas of a largely inhospitable terrain. Attempting to classify the peoples is a complex undertaking. Even the broadest of definitions beg to be qualified and this aspect is well illustrated if we look first to language as a means of distinguishing between communities.

The Indo-European family of languages embraces almost all those spoken in Europe and in the east the Indo-Aryan group, which includes Kurdish, Persian, Hindi, Assamese and Bengali. As long ago as the sixteenth century, Sanskrit was thought to be the 'mother' of European languages, but it was not until 1789 that Sir William Jones (1746-1794), a brilliant oriental linguist, provided scholarly confirmation that the links were stronger than could have possibly been produced by chance, citing the similarities to be found in the roots of verbs and forms of grammar. Within fifty years that great German philologist, Jakob Grimm, a founder of the study of comparative philology, had given his endorsement to the idea. The interest has been sustained, evinced as recently as 1968 with the publication of an Indo-European Grammar, a project directed by the Polish linguist Jerzy Kurlyowicz.

Among the five hundred or so Indo-Aryan languages spoken by about five hundred million people are to be found virtually all the languages spoken throughout the Himalayas: Pushtu, Assamese, Hindi, Urdu (meaning 'army' and the origin of the word 'horde'), Kashmiri (a mixture of Persian and Hindi), Nepali (related to Hindi), Bengali (related to Assamese), and many others where the distinction between language and dialect is by no means clear-cut. Tibetans speak a non-Indo-European tongue which has etymological links with Chinese, though the peoples are of different ethnic origin. Fascinating as speculation about common origins of language may be, at present it offers up more questions than it does answers to the identification of, and links between, ethnic communities along the Himalayan mountain chain.

The Sino-Tibetan group of languages, about which there is much controversy, highlights the interaction between language and geographical boundaries. 'Sino' refers to the Chinese dialect component and

'Tibetan' to the country where the language is spoken. Present borders between the Himalayan countries offer little help in the quest for ethnic groupings as they are all of relatively recent origin, and drawn for geographical reasons. Bhutan, for example, the kingdom which operates the memorably named national airline Thunder Dragon Air, is located between Tibet and Assam, the people speak a dialect of Tibetan, external affairs are guided by India, from which Bhutan receives much economic assistance. Sikkim was made independent in 1947, occupied by India in 1949 and became India's twenty-second state when the chogyal (king) abdicated in 1975; Tibetan is mostly spoken, although increasing numbers of immigrants from Nepal bring their own tongues. Nepal, the only country to adopt Hinduism as a national religion, has many ethnically distinguishable tribes speaking their own languages or dialects within borders that are well-established.

North India of the Himalayas, stretching from Jammu and Kashmir to Assam, contains a veritable hotch-potch of ethnic groups as diverse as the scenery, whilst to the west is the disputed region of Kashmir and the boundaries dividing India and Pakistan—-a particularly notable example of a political border separating peoples alike in language, culture and history. Kashmir, on the edge of the Karakorums and the Hindu Kush, holds together, in an uneasy proximity, Muslims, Hindus, Buddhists and Sikhs, living in a paradise on earth that, paradoxically, fathers religious hostility.

Religion in the Himalayas presents a relatively simple pattern which, beginning in the west, implants Islam from Afghanistan to Kashmir. Himachal Pradesh is largely Hindu, although there are Sikhs, the sizeable enclave of refugee Tibetan Buddhists living in exile in Dharamsala, the home of the Dalai Lama, and the Muslim Gujar in the Chamba Valley, bordering Jammu and Kashmir, who live by selling fresh milk and butter from their herds of buffalo. Uttar Pradesh is the veritable heartland of Hinduism, containing many of the most holy places of Hindu pilgrimage, but as a path is traced further east, so Hinduism blends with Buddhism. The former prevails along the lower and middle levels of mountains, whilst Buddhism has lodged in the heights and crossed into Tibet. Living in Assam, on the jungle slopes at the furthest eastern end of the Himalayas, are the Nagas, one of the most curious anomalies on earth. Tucked away in their dense rain forests where India, Tibet, Burma and China meet, they are largely Christian, speak English, and culturally resemble none of their neighbouring communities. There is a threat that their native Naga tongue could go the way of Latin, Sanskrit or proto-Indo-European, the language scholars suspect originated somewhere in the Urals, then spread into Europe and Asia to father so many offspring.

Space allows us to mention only a few of the many diverse peoples of the Himalayan region.

Pathans. Pathans, who speak Pushtu (or Pashto), an Iranian language, live in the North-West Frontier Province and the Federally Administered Northern Areas of Pakistan. There are about twelve million Pushtu-speaking Pakistanis, augmented by about three million refugees from Afghanistan: *melmastia* or hospitality, second in importance in the Pathan code of behaviour, has exerted a strong unifying influence among the Sunni Muslims. Pathans have always aroused a kind of wary respect among others. Taller, stronger and more active than most who live in the mountains, they probably drifted into Afghanistan and northern Pakistan from Iran thousands of years ago. Islam, Pushtu—-their language, and Paktunwali —-their code of behaviour, binds them together, but does not prevent the ferocious family feuds that are a permanent way of life. Until 1939, their bleak, barren homeland provided a vast training ground for the Indian Army against a dangerous adversary lodged along routes as celebrated in fact and fiction as the Khyber Pass. Experience gained by the Pathans no doubt contributed to the effective resistance met by the Soviet Army when they invaded so incautiously almost half a century later.

Kipling, in *Life's Little Handicaps*, writes a forceful paragraph on Pathan psychology: 'If from your earliest infancy you have been accustomed to look on battle, murder, and sudden death, if spilt blood affects your nerves as much as red paint, and, above all, if you have faithfully believed that the Bengali was the servant of all Hindustan, and that all Hindustan was vastly inferior to your own large, lustful self, you can endure...especially if your opponent's mother has frightened him to sleep in his youth with horrible stories of devils inhabiting Afghanistan...'

Sherpas. Smudged as the fringes of the ethnic miscellany may be, there are some races with a reputation as hill peoples that have left an indelible mark on the world's perception of them and their mountains. Best known, especially if their modest number of some forty thousand is taken into account, must be the Sherpas. Until Tenzing Norgay, personification of the admired characteristics of his people, stood on the peak of Everest, very little had been heard of them. As an aside, it has often puzzled people why there are no photographs taken by Tenzing of Hillary standing triumphant on Everest. In his book on their climb, Sir Edmund reveals that Tenzing had never taken a photograph, and the summit of the highest mountain in the world at 11.30 a.m. with a long climb downwards in prospect, 'seemed hardly the place to show him how'.

The Sherpas are usually Buddhist and speak Tibetan. Their name (*sha* = east, *pa* = people) explains their origin, which is the Tibetan plateau, from where they began to migrate to the Khumbu area south of Everest, settling in villages at around 10-13,000 ft (3-4,000 m.). Located astride a north-south trade route through high passes, centuries ago they established themselves as guides and porters who were willing to set aside their farming and livestock to help merchants passing through. From this it was a natural step to work at high altitude with the mountaineers who brought them their celebrity and gave young men an additional source of income. Their integrity, skill, energy, resourcefulness, trustworthiness and kindness to neighbours and animals have given them fame sufficient for the Ford Motor Company to name a van after them—-an accolade not lightly bestowed by western capitalism, so alert to the market's reaction.

Gurkhas. Gurkhas are not a single ethnic group, as is popularly supposed, but a variety of tribes: Gurung, Magar, Thakar, Rai, Limbu and Sunuwar, inhabiting an area mid-way between Kathmandu and Annapurna. The Gurungs, who make up the largest component of the Gurkhas, live in the fertile valleys of the Annapurna range. From well-kept villages in stunningly beautiful surroundings, they farm, keep sheep and enlist into the Indian and British armies, where their bravery, tenacity, humour and delight in soldiering have earned them universal respect.

As an eighteen-year-old National Serviceman in Malaya, I first saw their formidable weapon, the *kukri*, put to use when invited to a Dusshera, a religious festival held in September or October dedicated to the goddess of war, Durga. She was asked to bless the arms: mortars, machine-guns and rifles stacked for the occasion, and to grant the battalion success in battle. Around a biscuit-coloured square fringed by jungle palms, tall grass and an abundant mosaic of green forest, the Gurkhas had erected flat-roofed rattan shelters to give shade from the late-morning equatorial sun. Poultry and goats were despatched with one swift slash of a *kukri*, the distinctive Gurkha knife, some quite close to where I sat, and excitement mounted as an experienced soldier approached the single young buffalo on the parade-ground. All talk subsided into total silence, except for a whisper in my ear that a single clean strike from the *khora*, larger and stronger than normal *kukri*, was essential if the battalion was to ensure good luck in the coming year.

Any reservations I might have had about animal sacrifice and the smell of blood on the hot sand had long been submerged by generous glasses of cold beer, which I drank before noon for the first time in my life. Moreover, the infectious excitement of the occasion, the brazenly pagan exultation of what being a Gurkha meant in that assembly, left no room for feeling squeamish. A well-muscled young man, taut-faced and fully aware of the responsibility resting on his bronzed, sweating shoulders, positioned himself with precision and patience. All his tension flowed into the quickest and cleanest of blows that left the animal standing momentarily as its head fell to the dust. The accumulating anxiety in that community of men-at-arms abruptly burst into an exultant howl of their famous war-cry *'Ayo Gurkhali'*, and the characteristic grins supplanted the unfamiliar apprehensiveness.

I have a poor quality black-and-white photograph as a memento. Just as well, for, emotionally drained by the episode and overwhelmed by the hospitality, I had to make an early departure. Judging by the contained amusement it occasioned, this was not wholly unexpected and was solicitously attributed to the excessive humidity. My head the next morning left me in no doubt that the glasses of chilled lager, so readily imbibed, were not entirely blameless in the matter of my premature leave-taking.

The long-standing military association goes back to the early nineteenth century, when the East India Company found a militant Nepal on its northern border and sent a punitive expedition in four columns against it. Only after two years of campaigning did the war end, when a vastly larger army drove the Nepalese back to Kathmandu. Respect for the other side was mutual, and so began the British recruitment of Gurkhas, whose allegiance has been as unflinching as their bravery.

Like all people who live in mountains, they have a mettle that engenders admiration. In the towns of the plains, their clothes, accents and unfeigned amazement when confronted with unfamiliar objects of urban civilisation may amuse the same people who know that in the mountains, hill-men survive in an often hostile environment. Often, but not always; for there are the valleys where wheat, barley, millet, maize, apricots, mustard, bananas, grapes and melons are grown; there are orchards of apples, peaches, mulberries and pears; on moist hillsides, rice is grown among streams gathering to go to their mother-rivers.

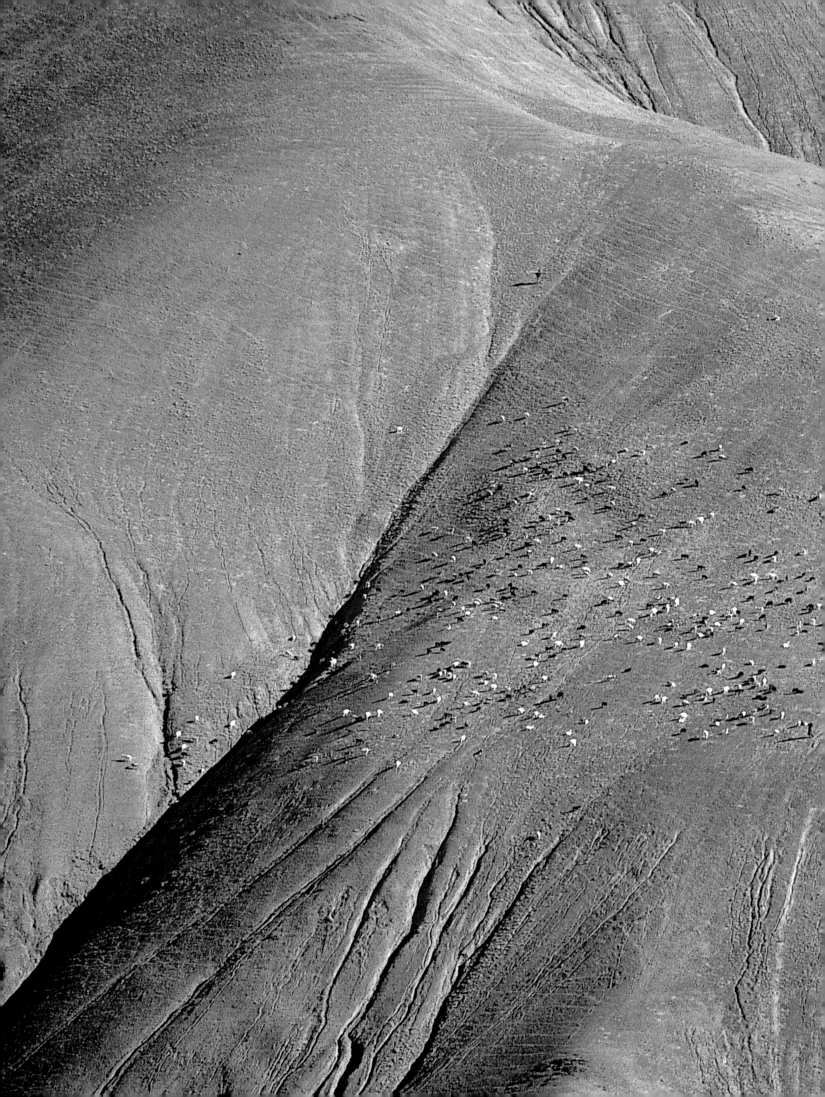

21. Shepherd boys tend a flock of goats
on the steep slopes above the village of
Rumbagh on the way to the Marka Valley.

22. A youngster from Rumbagh during
the milking of the goats and sheep that
are all important to the village economy.

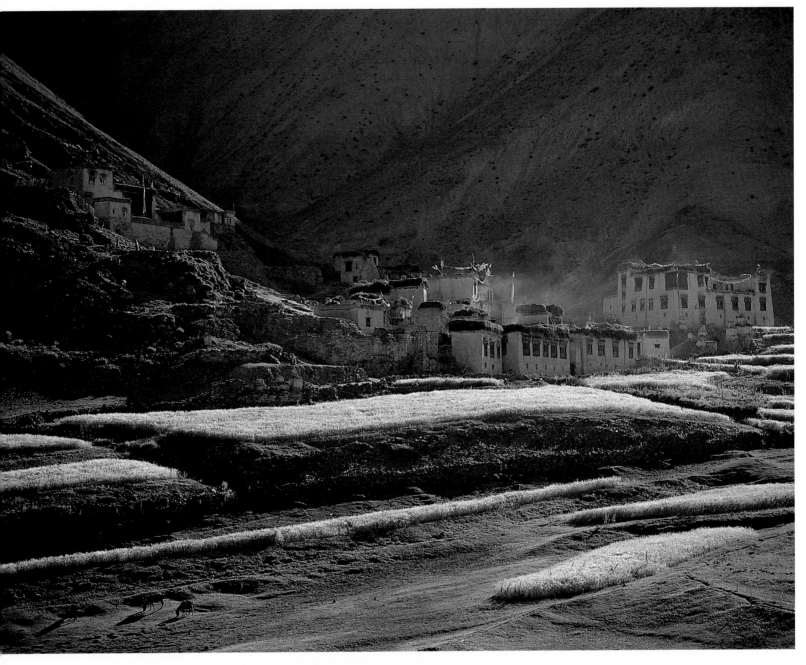

23. The village of Rumbagh, tucked away in a branch off the main valley leading to the Ganda La Pass (5,000 m.), is a day's walk from the Indus Valley.

24. A typical interior of a Buddhist house in the village of Chilling above the Zanskar River, decorated by numerous cooking pots ranged on wooden shelves.

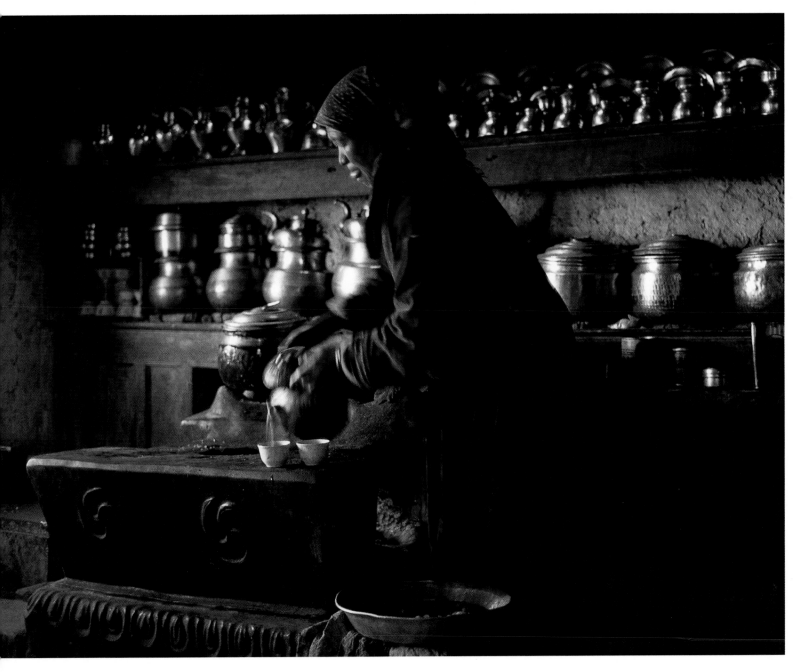

*25. A Ladakhi housewife making tea,
which is drunk in the morning with
'tsampa' (parched barley meal).
Vegetable soup, apricots, 'dhal' (lentils)
and 'bhat' (rice) are other common items
in the local diet.*

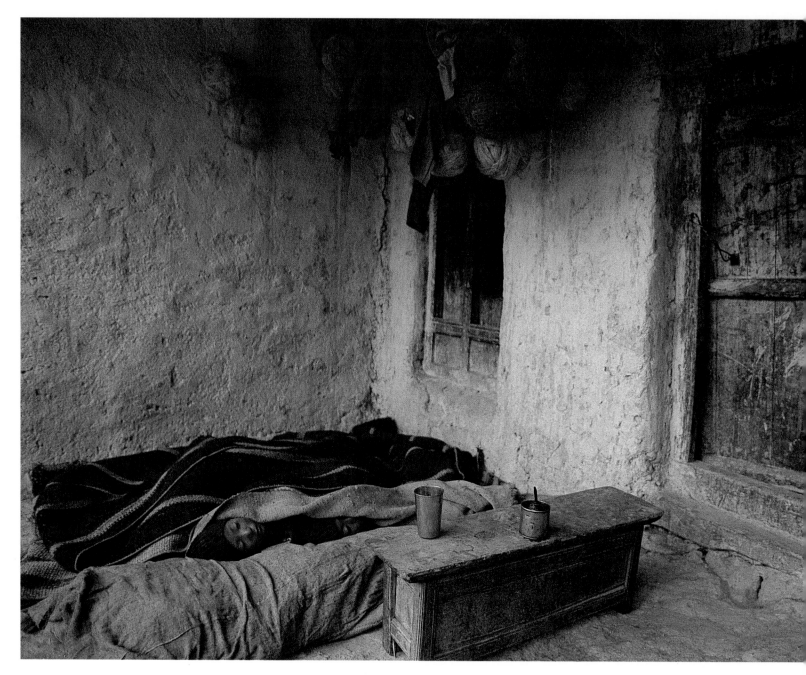

26. If the family is large, it is not unusual for some of the children to sleep outside in the yard, with only a projecting roof over their heads. Before they fall asleep, the mother takes care they are warmly covered with homespun blankets.

27. These village children seem to be supporting the slogan 'Free Ladakh', a reminder of the conflicts between Muslims and Buddhists: Ladakh is part of predominantly Muslim Kashmir.

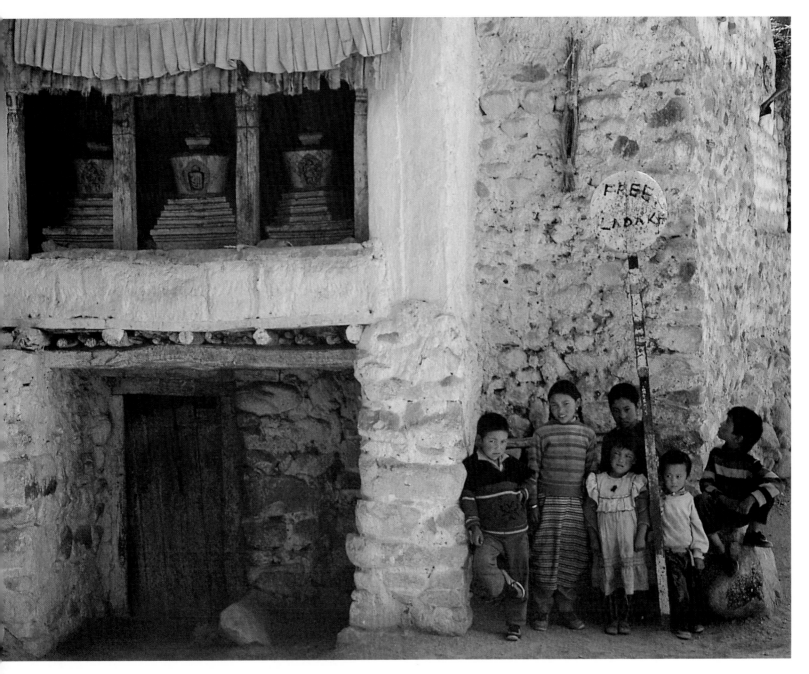

28. A Ladakhi woman playing with her one-year-old daughter while making butter tea (overleaf). This traditional type of Ladakhi tea, called 'solja', is made with salt and butter and tastes more like a soup.

29. Ladakhi women winnowing wheat at the end of September. Women here, as in other parts of the Himalayan region, do their full share of heavy farm work for as long as they are physically capable. (pp. 50-51)

30. Thikse Gompa, one of the most impressive monasteries in the Indus Valley, was established by the Gelugpa order in the fifteenth century. The monks' quarters stretch right across the hillside topped by the main building.

31. Leh Gompa stands above the palace and overlooks the ruins of the older palace of the king of Tagpebums. In all, there are three monasteries on the hill.

32. A Muslim girl from Ladakh (overleaf). Among the predominantly Buddhist population there is a Muslim minority, most of them Kashmiri merchants and their families.

33. A Ladakhi woman spinning sheep's wool on a twirling distaff. She wears a 'perak', a head-dress of rough-cut turquoises, which can have three, five, seven or nine rows of stones, depending on the rank of the wearer. (p. 55)

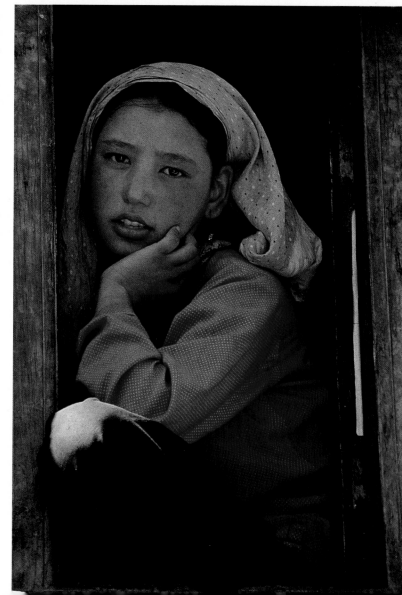

34. A Ladakhi wearing a 'goucha', a thick woollen robe tied at the waist with a colourful sash known as a 'skera'.

35. Many Ladakhis are nomads who follow their herds of goats. This charming girl (top) encountered on the road from Kargil to Leh belongs to one such nomadic group.

36. A young Ladakhi girl poses in the window of a house in the old centre of Leh, below the palace.

37-39. The Ladakhis, who are of the
Tibetan-Mongol physical type, are a
healthy-looking people, deep brown in
colouring due to the strong summer sun.
They are also a happy people and their
native greeting, 'Juley', is friendly and
spontaneous. Their neighbours often
refer to them as 'smiling faces'.

40, 41. Young novices at a school for monks in Hemis Gompa. It is usually the youngest son in a Buddhist family who becomes a monk, but there is no strict rule about this: any son can do so, provided his father gives consent. This will depend on the family's needs: some must stay at home to help run the farm and look after the rest of the family.

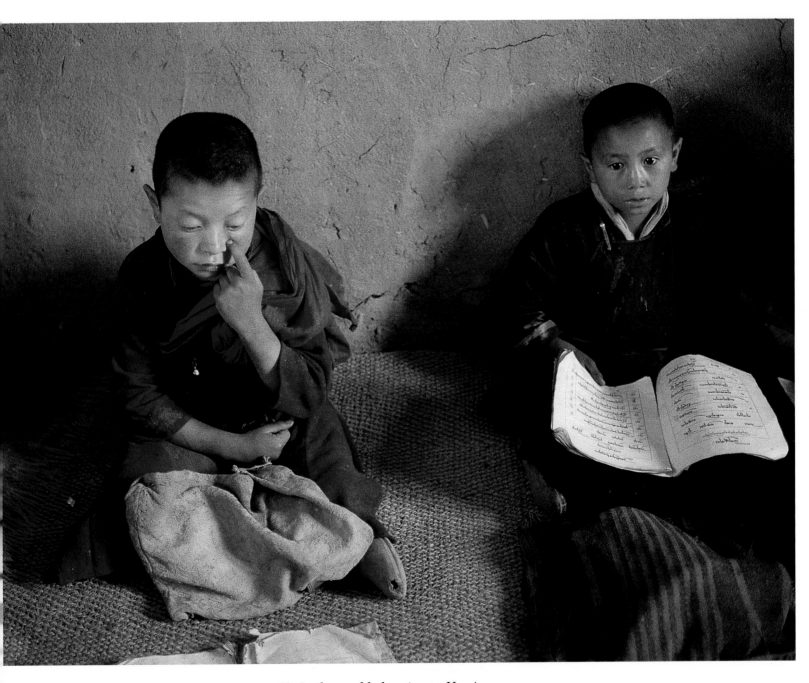

42. *In the yard belonging to Hemis Gompa (overleaf), a nun is preparing to make 'tsampa', parched barley meal, which forms part of the frugal diet. Some monastic communities, like this one, include nuns as well as monks. There are also separate nunneries.*

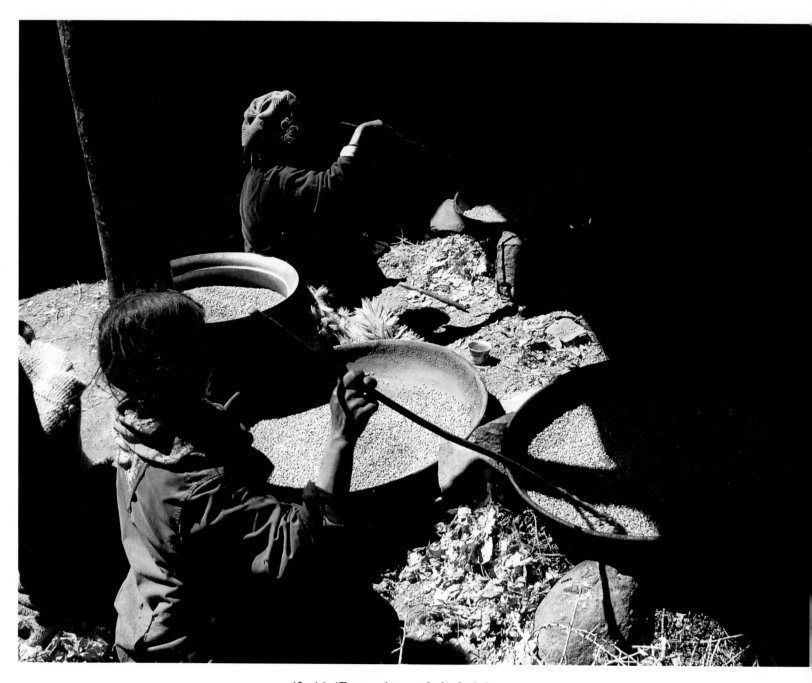

43, 44. 'Tsampa' is made by lightly
roasting barley in a large metal pan, with
some sand added to prevent the barley
catching alight. The barely is then sieved
to remove the sand and the roasted grain
is ground in a water-driven mill.

45. *A novice at Hemis Gompa. Boys destined for a monastic life usually enter a monastery at around the age of six. Nearly every family gives one son.*

46. *While a nun is busy with the 'tsampa', a monk is preparing 'chang', the local beer brewed from barley and millet which gets its specific flavour from the addition of pepper and sugar.*

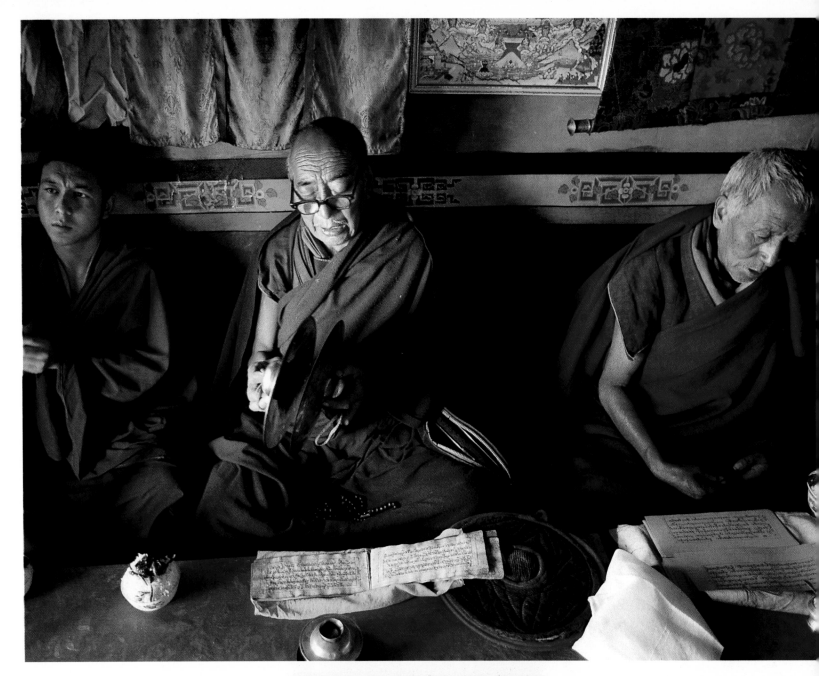

47. Monks usually minister to the spiritual needs of villagers. In this household, a son had died in a car accident one month before, and three lamas were called in to exorcise demons. They conducted the rites in the family's roof-top shrine.

48. A novice in Thikse Gompa pours butter tea into a monk's cup during the morning prayers.

49. A monk at the elaborately ornamented doors of the Lakhang shrine at Hemis Gompa.

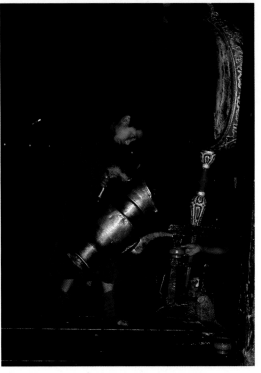

50. A novice at Shey Gompa (overleaf) observes the smile of enlightenment of the largest golden Buddha statue in Ladakh, worked in gold and gilded copper sheets. Standing 12 m. high, it was erected by King Dalden Nangyal in the mid-seventeenth century.

51. A fresco at Shey Gompa illustrating the Buddha legend. Such frescoes usually cover the walls of chambers that contain a statue of the Buddha. (pp. 70-71)

*52, 53. Alchi Choskor, one of the ancient
monasteries of Ladakh, was built in the
eleventh century by Lotsava Rinchen
Zangpo. He invited many famous artists
from Kashmir and Tibet, who decorated
the walls with paintings of different
mandalas which have deep tantric
interpretations.*

54. In the library of Shey Gompa: a novice is singing in front of the 'book shelves'.

55. A book printed from woodcuts in the library of Shey Gompa, chronicling the lives of Buddhist saints. When not in use by the monks, its bark-paper pages are pressed between lacquered slats bound by a silk brocade ribbon.

56. Fresco in a chapel which houses an enormous 15-metre-

high figure of the seated Buddha at Thikse Gompa.

57, 58. The Lakhang Soma of Hemis Gompa contains manifestations of Bodhisattva Manjushri. All the walls are covered with dense rows of tiny Buddhas and Bodhisattvas surrounding a central motif that repeats in larger format the figure depicted on that particular wall. In all, there are 364 representations of Manjushri on the walls. (pp. 76-79)

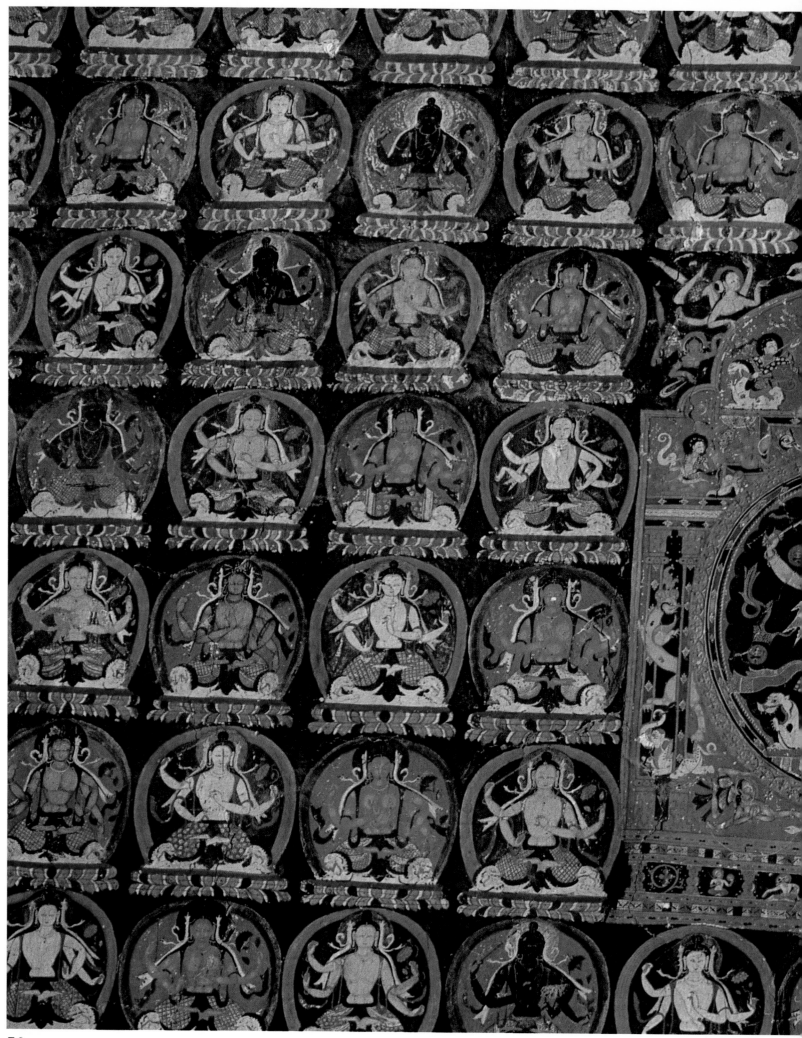

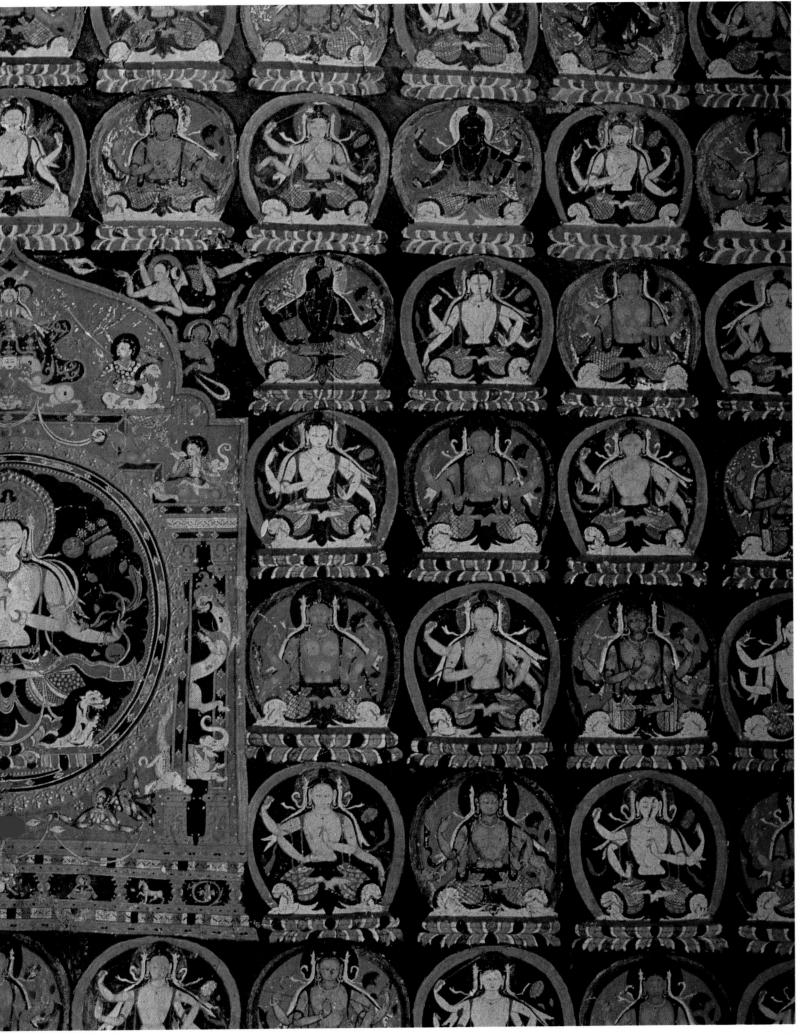

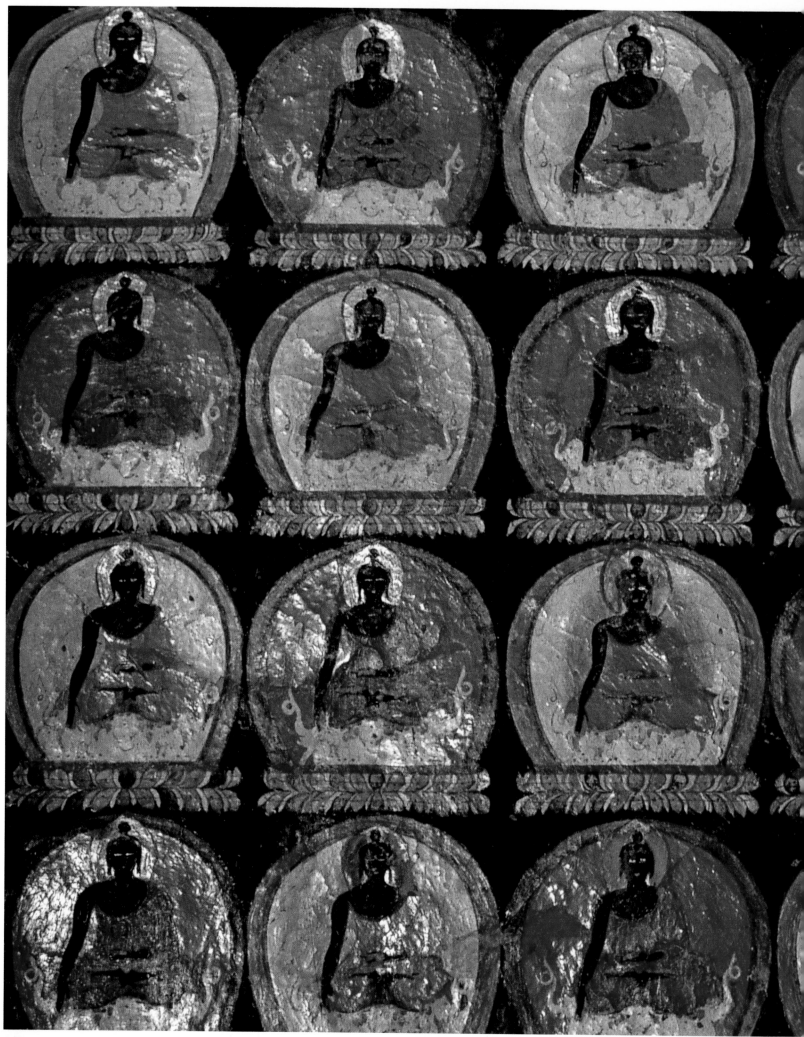

In his novel *Kim*, Rudyard Kipling caught the contrast between the plains-dweller, Kim, and the hill-man, the Lama, in this memorable passage: 'Kim had all the plainsman's affection for the well-trodden track, not six feet wide, that snaked among the mountains; but the Lama, being Tibetan, could not refrain from the short-cuts over spurs and the rims of gravel-strewn slopes. As he explained to his limping disciple, a man bred among mountains can prophesy the course of a mountain road, and though low-lying clouds might be a hindrance to a short-cutting stranger, they made no earthly difference to a thoughtful man...'

Says the Lama, later: ' "These are the hills of my delight! Shadows blessed above all other shadows! Here my eyes opened on this world... Out of the Hills I came—the high Hills and the strong winds. Oh, just is the Wheel." He blessed them in detail—the great glaciers, the naked rocks, the piled moraines and tumbled shale; dry upland, hidden salt-lake, age-old timber and fruitful water-shot valley one after the other, as a dying man blesses his fold; and Kim marvelled at his passion.'

Kafir-Kalash. Of all the hill-people, the Bhotias, Durranis, Gurungs, Hazara, Hunzakuts, Kazakhs, Kashmiri, Lepcha, Nagars, Newari, Nuristanis, Pathans, Sherpas and Tibetans, the most immediately intriguing are the Kafir-Kalash. Numbering some three thousand or so, they dwell west of Chitral and make up an isolated pocket of animal and nature worshippers surrounded by Muslims. However, if conversion to Islam fails, as it has failed for a thousand years or more, then transformation by tourism is a possibility.

Kafir-Kalash (Wearers of Black Robes) look more Aryan than most hill-peoples: they are often fair-skinned and/or light-haired, and some have blue eyes. Obviously, such a curious enclave provokes questions, chief among them: how did the Kafir-Kalash come to the mountains? They themselves believe they are descended from a general in the army of Alexander the Great who settled in Chitral. The women finger-weave their homespun clothes; they wear many and long necklaces, numerous bangles and pendant earrings. In the summer they don small round pill-box caps and in winter a head-dress that hangs down to the waist at the back, and is intricately worked with glass beads, cowrie shells, stones, buttons and tiny bells. Their houses, built of cedar-wood and stone, contain chairs—-rare among hill-people, who generally squat on the floor. Their religion, to which they have so tenaciously clung, is a curious mixture of animal and nature worship. Their lunar calendar begins in March, and includes a Month of Teats, denoting the birth of animals in the spring season.

Kafiristan, where they live, was conquered in 1895 by the Emir Abdur Rahman Khan Ghazi, whereupon all the inhabitants were converted to Islam. To mark this, the name of the area was changed from Kafiristan (Country of Unbelievers) to Nuristan (Country of Light). The area, but not the Kafir-Kalash, is described in Eric Newby's travel classic *A Short Walk in the Hindu Kush* and in Rudyard Kipling's *The Man Who Would be King*, a romantic tale of an isolated mountain kingdom where a couple of adventurous British soldiers cheerfully accept divine status.

Inevitably, international curiosity about such a group of ethnic non-conformists is likely to attract increasing sociological research and

59. The old palace of the kings of Ladakh overlooking the town of Leh from the south-east slope of Tsemo Hill. It was built by King Singe Namgyal in the sixteenth century, about the same time as the famous Potala in Lhasa, which it resembles. Like the Shey Palace, the one in Leh still belongs to the Ladakhi royal family, who now live in their palace in Stok.

tourism, neither of which promises to leave this Himalayan anomaly unchanged much longer. On the other hand, any social system capable of surviving all the rigours of life in the Hindu Kush and all the persecutions that have taken place there, should be able to withstand the intrusion of curious outsiders.

Religions

Hinduism. Hinduism, characterised by its kaleidoscope of perplexing gods and goddesses, maintains in its ritual chants or mantras that the origins of the world began in the vast Himalayan shrine. Inspiration for the Hindu tradition can be geographically pinpointed to Mount Kailas, 22,022 ft (6,714 m.), located around the middle of the Himalayan range in western Tibet and some 100 miles (160 km.) from the northern border of Nepal. The area is notable for more than its awesome ice-ridged peaks; nearby are gold fields and Lake Manasarowar, 14,950 ft (4,558 m.) above sea level, probably the highest expanse of fresh water in the world. The locality is also a watershed for four of the largest and most vital waterways on the subcontinent: the rivers Indus, Sutlej, Ganges and Brahmaputra. Kailas is well below the highest point in the Himalayas but the area is the most sacred in the eyes of the Hindus, Buddhists and the devotees of Bon, Tibet's indigenous religion.

Rosters of gods, deities, spirits, saints and divines, along with monasteries, temples, stupas and tombs, satisfy spiritual needs throughout the vast mountain chain, but Kailas and its surroundings have a special significance as the source of the holy Ganges. Fusing the divine and temporal, the watercourse sustains those living along its flood-plain and offers salvation to the Hindu who is immersed three times in its turgid waters or whose funeral ashes are cast upon the surface. Shiva—one of the three gods, Brahma, Shiva and Vishnu, which dominate the Hindu pantheon— sits on his throne on Kailas with the matted locks of his hair flowing all around him. From one of these strands, it is believed, the holy Ganges issues and from this cosmological centre of the earth the Hindu gods embrace the heavens and guide humanity. Although, rather charmingly, not without provoking an irreverent quatrain which runs:

'The Goddess Lotus sleeps in the lotus calix,
Shiva on the Himalayas,
Vishnu on the Milky Ocean,
This they do, I suppose, for fear of bedbugs.'

Hinduism gets off to a bad start in the eyes of many non-Hindus because of its emphasis on idolatry. Yet, with all its attendant illusions, it has gained and maintained a kind of truth. For thousands of years it has satisfied the spiritual needs of countless millions of people. To endure, a religion, like much else, has to be able to adapt. Original dogma has to withstand variations proposed by mystics from within, as well as social change from without, whilst continuing to offer comfort and solace for the inevitable way of all flesh. No student of Hinduism can fail to recognise the manner in which it has absorbed contrary views, adapted to change and given faith to its devotees.

The north of India has been a perennial battleground over which mighty conquerors, and more modest raiders, have rampaged, but Hinduism, like the Himalayas themselves, has provided a combination of physical and spiritual refuge. Although it has no fixed scriptural canon, there are ancient philosophical texts such as the *Vedas* (Sanskrit: divine knowledge) which were composed by the Aryans who invaded the sub-continent from an area on the north-west fringe of the Himalayas. Their preservation is due to a meticulous oral tradition which took rigid care over pronunciation and, by laying stress on the sacredness of the language, resisted translation. Memorising and reciting the *Vedas* is still an act of religious merit, although the actual practices have been supplanted by later Hindu doctrine. Fundamental to these scriptures, which originated around 1400 B.C. and were written down seven centuries later, is the celebration of nature, worshipped through the gods: Indra (rain and thunder), Agni (fire), Surya (sun) and Soma (the god of the plant from which an intoxicating drink was distilled). From these remote beginnings came Brahminism, which introduced the idea of a universal spirit, Brahma, the Creator, accompanied by Vishnu, the Preserver, and Shiva, the Destroyer and Reproducer.

This cosmotheism has never been easily understood by outsiders, and since the Hindu religion can only be practised by those born into Hindu families, there is no attempt to win converts. Moreover, there is no one temple greater than others, such as St. Peter's in Rome, no one priest above all others, such as the pope, no central administration which co-ordinates worship, rules on varying interpretations of scripture and gives authoritative coherence to, or guidance on, religious matters. This absence of one central voice makes for a flexible faith for an exclusive community. The attitude a century ago of anyone enquiring into Hinduism is typically summed up in the words of Sir Alfred Lyall, a contributor to the Bengal Census Report in 1881: 'The religion of the non-Mohammedan population of India is a tangled jungle of disorderly superstitions, ghosts and demons, demi-gods and deified saints, household gods, local gods, tribal gods, universal gods, with their countless shrines and temples, and the din of their discordant rites; deities who abhor a fly's death; those who still delight in human sacrifices.'

Some forty years before Sir Alfred confided his puzzlement to a report, another commentator, Thomas Babington Macauley, raged against a practice far worse than honouring a host of multi-faceted gods: the Hindu rite of widow-burning, or *suttee*: 'It is lamentable to think how long after our power was firmly established in Bengal, we, grossly neglecting the first and plainest duty of the civil magistrate, suffered the practices of infanticide and *suttee* to continue unchecked.'

This unacceptable face of Hinduism, which could involve hundreds of wives of one ruler, was later suppressed. But it was not until 1955 and 1956 that Indian legislation gave inheritance rights to widows and daughters and permitted divorce.

The caste system, too, has always attracted criticism despite being recognised as part of an enduring social system (rather than a religion) accepted by 600 million Indians. Caste began with the acceptance of *dharma* (truth) and *karma* (proper behaviour), as well as the four classes: Brahmins (priests), Ksatryas (nobles or warriors), Vaisya (tradesmen) and Shudras (labourers), who sprang respectively from the Supreme Being's mouth, arms, thighs and feet. A fifth caste, the untouchables (*pariah* or *panchamas*) are excluded from the system. Such a rigid classification of mankind contains little to attract contemporary westerners, having overtones of the Nazi Party which, interestingly enough, chose the ancient Sanskrit symbol of the swastika as an emblem in 1920, and in 1930 decreed it should become the German flag.

Mahatma Gandhi, that austere reformer and shrewd politician, tried hard to attract Muslim support but could never entirely escape from Hindu values, which, ironically, led to his assassination at the hands of a Hindu fanatic in January 1948, a year after partition. The slaughter and pillage which accompanied the partition of India and Pakistan left behind a distrustful sub-continent which persists to this day.

Undoubtedly the caste system is now crumbling, particularly in the northern cities. I remember escorting an unsteady senior Brahmin to his car and chauffeur after he had dined and drunk rather liberally at my house. He remarked that his steps were somewhat erratic and when I asked, genuinely curious about the religious implications, whether he would have to perform some penance, he halted, placed a steadying hand on my shoulder, and smiled confidingly: 'One of the better parts about being a Brahmin is that I cannot be contaminated; instead, pollutants are purified by coming into contact with me. Just think of all the good I have done tonight.' I could still hear his laughter from the back seat of his car as the tail lights vanished, and wondered how much longer this exclusive birthright could continue.

Humankind has, of course, often thought along similar lines and Hinduism, a religion coming down from Himalayan altars which dwarf all others, has survived assault from outside and within. Muslim monotheistic invaders were particularly savage on followers of a faith worshipping a mega family of gods, although it must be said the savagery

Varuna, the ancient Hindu God of the Sky and Cosmic Order, later the God of Water.

Tara the Saviouress, a Tantric Buddhist female deity especially popular in Tibet and Nepal.

fluctuated with the tolerance of various Mogul emperors.

Sikhism. Sikhism, a kind of synthesis of Hinduism and Islam, reacted against Hindu ritual and the caste system, and recognised the inspiration of Mohammed, yet it helped to preserve Hinduism against the rule of the Muslims, who dominated the north of India from the thirteenth century until British colonial rule was established around the middle of the nineteenth century. Sikhism began with the teachings of Nanak (1469-1539), the first of the ten gurus. From the last, Gobind Singh (1666-1708), came the concept of *Singh* and *Kaur* for men and women respectively, as well as the symbols of their faith worn by all Sikh men, the five Ks: *Kesh* (uncut beard and hair), *Kangha* (comb, to keep their hair clean beneath the turban), *Kara* (metal bracelet), *Kaccha* (knee-length underpants) and *Kirpan* (dagger). As the symbols suggest, Sikhism is rather more temporal than spiritual; its most holy of shrines is the Golden Temple at Amritsar (late sixteenth century), rather than the celestial Himalayas.

The *Rigveda*, the first of the sacred books of the *Vedas,* is older than Homer, and Hinduism has proved infinitely more enduring as a moral and spiritual guide to far more people than most faiths. Marxism, by comparison, which has arguably had a bigger impact on the world than any other belief since Islam, has notably failed to excite lasting interest in emphatically materialistic goals. Hinduism's 'failure' is that it does not travel well outside India's borders, and some of those who have endeavoured to bring it westward have achieved lucrative success at odds with the spiritual concepts surrounding disciplines such as transcendental meditation; to the loss of credibility in the latter. Whilst the western pilgrims who journeyed to Kashmir along the hippy-trail to its Kathmandu terminus in the 1970s may have felt themselves in the presence of some disturbing truth, their experiences often owed something to marijuana, then on sale at little more than the price of walnuts.

I lived in India in the mood of the pilgrim. Like so many, I wondered whether the ancient East had any answer to contemporary complexities. In recent decades, millions in the West believe that they have found a remedy in yogaic exercise, an exportable facet of Hinduism, usually bereft of its ritual purpose of achieving union with Brahma. Latterly, yoga (the word means union) seems to have lost ground to exercise routines set to bass-amplified dance rhythms as a true path to physical and mental well-being. My personal search for a more alert centre of consciousness was tested early during an encounter with a renowned ascetic who closely examined my right hand. He was obviously nonplussed by a set of callouses likely to be found on the hand of an indigenous labourer but out of place on the palm and fingers of an apparently prosperous foreigner (after all, I could afford his fee). His psychic powers stopped short at recognising the blemishes acquired playing tennis.

Scepticism, however, comes less easily in the mountains. For the people of the Himalayas, prayer and worship are an immemorial passion. Their domain is a vast fortress, turreted, ramparted, bridged and moated, where roam the spirits of avalanches, sudden clouds and raging gales. They recognise the responsibility and risk of cohabitation in the stronghold of capricious gods. Their monasteries, temples and shrines are frontier posts, a half-way house between rampaging invaders and the abode of those same gods. Man, so alone in all this emptiness, cannot but cling to the belief that he is the agent of some much greater spirit. If the Himalayas have left any legacy to mankind, it is spirituality, ways of thinking about birth, life, truth, humanity and death.

Buddhism. Unlike Hinduism, Buddhism was not born in the Himalayas, but it did successfully cross the mountains, establish itself on their sides and extend eastwards as far as Japan and Korea.

The origins of Buddhism embrace the four principal events in the life of Prince Siddhartha Gautama (?563-483 B.C.?): his birth, enlightenment (Buddha = The Enlightened One), first preaching and decease. These took place respectively at Lumbini, Bodh-Gaya, Sarnath and Kushinagar, all of which are regarded as places of great sanctity. He was born and brought up in luxury, but at the age of twenty-nine, when he saw an old man, a sick man and a corpse, the Prince realised that he, too, would grow old, become infirm and die. After fruitlessly seeking understanding of the human condition from two leading Brahmins, he meditated beneath a bo-tree at Bodh-Gaya until, resisting attempts to make him return to his customary world, he became the Buddha.

At Sarnath he preached his first sermon and subsequently devoted his life to teaching, mostly in what is now the Indian state of Bihar. He attracted many disciples to what was a wandering religious order which established nucleic communities among a largely Hindu population. In Kushinagar, aged almost eighty, the greatly revered Buddha died, his cremation being conducted with befitting pomp and his ashes distributed among the peoples to whom he had preached.

When he died, Buddhism was the religion of a reforming sect practised by relatively few people. Hinduism and Buddhism existed side by side, sharing some gods, attitudes and religious sites. Stripped of the forest of idols and cleared of the undergrowth of predestination by virtue of caste, the Buddhist modification of Hinduism offered a highly acceptable path to salvation.

Buddhism is firmly imbued in the teachings and personality of the Buddha. There is no Supreme God. Gautama taught that nothing exists permanently; there is only, in his somewhat pessimistic view, change and decay. To have any chance of happiness we must accept the fact that attachment to people or possessions eventually brings misery. The attainment of salvation and a higher life is possible, but does not rest with the gods; it depends on man himself. A 'middle path' between worldliness and asceticism is possible if a man achieves detachment by means of the intense mental discipline of meditation. This, in turn, brings about enlightenment and a cessation of the cycle of lives.

Four Noble Truths succinctly define the essence of Buddhism:
To exist is to suffer.
Suffering arises from greed and attachment to the impermanent.
Suffering stops if attachment ceases.
Following the Eightfold Path will end the suffering.

The Eightfold Path charts the passage to wisdom and includes: right understanding, attitude, speech, behaviour, occupation, effort, state of mind and meditation. The principal virtues embraced by Buddhism are charity, compassion, truthfulness, chastity, regard for monasteries, and self-restraint. Respect for all these can lead to *nirvana* or supreme bliss.

Buddha's faith became known as Theravada Buddhism (Teaching of the Elders) and is today found mainly in Sri Lanka, Cambodia, Thailand and other south-east Asian countries. Its lofty ideals have done much for Asian civilisation where they have held sway, and generated respect where they have not. Even in India, which dismissed Buddhism, the final rejection was by the flattering form of absorption. A Theravadian monk is strictly disciplined by eating solely food that is given him, observing celibacy and not harming living beings. Only with the development of martial arts in Japan did Buddhism tolerate an element of militancy, in contrast to the monk-knights of Christianity, the assassins of Islam and the militarist order of the Sikhs. Monastic routine forbids the ownership of worldly possessions and concentrates on Buddhist teachings, including control of the mind through yoga or meditation.

In the first century A.D. a less austere form, Mahayana (Great Vehicle) Buddhism, which allowed worship before other gods and goddesses, evolved and spread to Nepal, Tibet, China, Korea and Japan. Mahayanists recognise several Buddhas and Bodhisattvas (near-Buddhas who postpone their nirvana to help others). They also hold the sophisticated religious concept that, since everything is impermanent, even Buddhist doctrines, followers should not become too dependent upon them. Far less spiritual, it might seem, is the Zen (meditation) sect, which influenced the unfolding of martial arts in Japan.

Lamaism. Another subsect, the Gelugpa, gained prominence in Tibet. Their leader, the Dalai (Ocean of Wisdom) Lama, is the God King, at present living in exile in India. Panchen (Great Scholar) Lama is a title that originated in the seventeenth century and was bestowed upon the abbot of the Tashilumpo Monastery. The present holder lives and works in Beijing. Whereas Buddhism in India by merging into Hinduism was lost from sight around 1200 A.D., Lamaist Buddhism in Tibet flourished until the People's Liberation Army of the Chinese Communists, having vanquished the Kuomintang (Nationalist) forces of Chiang Kai-shek, entered Lhasa in 1951. By 1959 Chinese rule in Tibet had become so intolerable the Dalai Lama fled to India, where he and other Tibetans were given refuge by the Indian Government. Chinese 're-education' which followed focused closely upon several thousand monasteries and the monks, nuns and lamas (spiritual teachers), who contributed little to the nation's economy, whilst Chinese resources financed new roads, hospitals and schools.

A Tibetan carpet-seller in New Delhi once made a penetrating comment on the situation as we sat among his thick, brilliantly-dyed wares and, as is the custom, turned momentarily aside from the litany of bargaining to speculate on broader issues. I asked about conditions in his homeland. Sitting cross-legged in a Buddha-like triangulation, he ran a massaging hand along the calloused sole of his foot and with all the controlled alertness of the bazaar trader down from the hills, well aware a profitable sale could result from the precise use of the right words, he solemnly reflected as he gazed obliquely beneath lowered eye-lids, 'Your poet put it: "East is East and Further East is Further East, and never the two shall meet".' We laughed together and the handshake which followed indicated both my amusement and my acknowledgement that his price was the one I would pay, honouring those timeless lubricants of commerce: a bargain, politics, intelligence and good-humour.

Three particular concepts provided an enduring basis for the establishment and expansion of Buddhism. First were the sanghas, or monasteries, whose communities of mendicant monks could live together and meditate in places made sacred by their Master's enlightenment and sermons. Second were the stupas (places of offerings), tall hemispheres of stone or clay. Eight of the earliest contained the ashes of the Buddha and subsequently they were constructed to house the ashes of his most enlightened followers. The stupa is as fundamental and distinguished a symbol of Buddhism as the cross is to Christianity. In China and Japan, it evolved in attenuated form as the elegant pagoda. Different parts of the stupa represent the elements: the base is associated with the earth, the dome with water, and the shaft with fire; at the top is the half-moon for air and a globe for the sun and heavens. The sum of the parts is a Path to Enlightenment. The third concept, pilgrimage, bound the others together. So universal has been the appeal of pilgrimage that it became an important act of piety for Christians, while one of the four principal duties of a Muslim is to make the *haj* to Mecca.

Whatever the merits of Buddhist teachings, the allure of the monasteries, architectural attraction of the stupa and enduring fascination of pilgrimage, it was the conversion of King Ashoka of India (273-232 B.C.) which effectively launched the new 'religion', leading to the building of innumerable stupas and the dispatch of missions to China, Sri Lanka and the West. The Mauriya Emperor regarded his imperial calling as a humanitarian mission. Through his royal patronage, a minor sect devoted to monastic reform became a great secular religion, and in the process helped to unify his far-flung empire. From his impetus Buddhism would flourish in India until the seventh century A.D., when Hindu revivalism re-established the old faith. By the eleventh century the military penetration of the Muslim conquest led to the sacking of temples as well as the suppression of any faith other than Islam. Given the ruthless intolerance of the invaders, it is all the more remarkable that temples and statuary did survive and that Buddhism crossed the formidable passes of the Himalayas to root elsewhere.

Little expresses the sobering fascination of the corrugated Himalayas better than the places of pilgrimage. These scattered examples of unrecorded virtuoso engineering embellished with religious artefacts demand devout muscularity of the pious. Perhaps, in places, the odour of sanctity increasingly gives way to the recognition of tourism, and the oversight of the caretakers falls short of the imagination of the fabricators, yet still they bestow some of the most memorable revelations of travel. It is possible to feel a supplicant in a land of hallucination, but there is also a feeling that a search for truth and reality persists at altitudes where gods, goddesses, saints and demons beckon. And to most of us agnostic, unenlightened cyphers of the market culture, environmentally alert humanists perhaps, but spiritually detached, the high drama of that serrated theatre in the Himalayas is all the more compelling, whilst the prevalent acceptance that death is only a temporary end to a familiar pattern is disturbingly humbling.

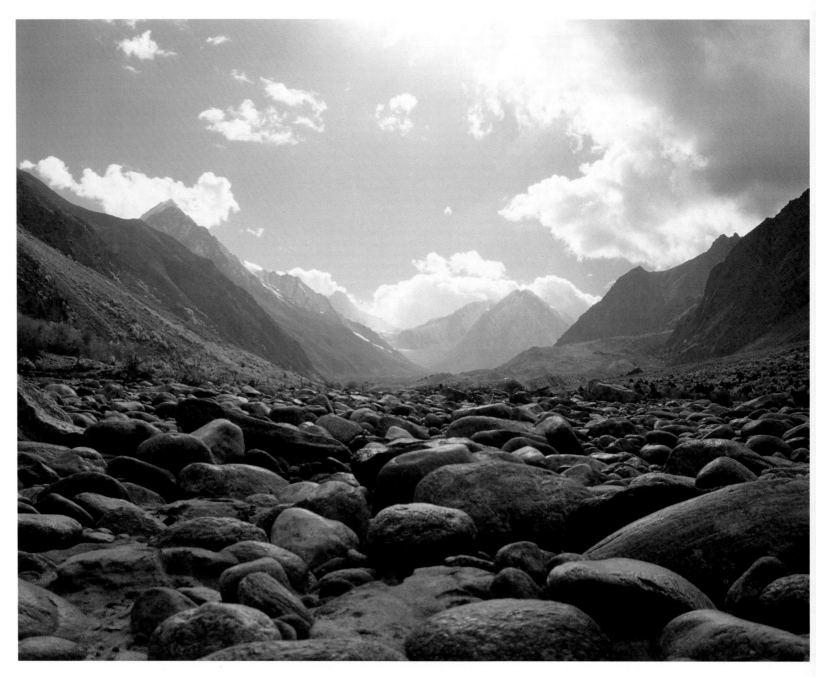

*62. View eastward from the Rupal Valley
towards Indian Kashmir, part of the state
of Jammu and Kashmir, which has a
population of some eight million.*

*63. On the south-west spur of Nanga
Parbat, at an altitude of around 6,000 m,
the view opens towards the mountains
bordering on India.*

64. An elderly Kashmiri carrying wood for his home in the village of Tereshing from the distant areas of the upper Rupal Valley. Firewood is scarce locally, and gathering it requires long treks over rough terrain.

65. With the coming of winter, Kashmiri shepherds leave the upland grazing for their homes in the valley.

66. *As one follows the Gujar nomadic trails to the meadow at Shock Dharan, a wonderful view opens up of the snow-capped mountain range on the opposite side of the valley.*

67. The snow-powdered slopes of the mountains reflected in the clear waters of Lake Krishansar, a two-day walk from Sonamarg in the Sindh Valley, Kashmir.

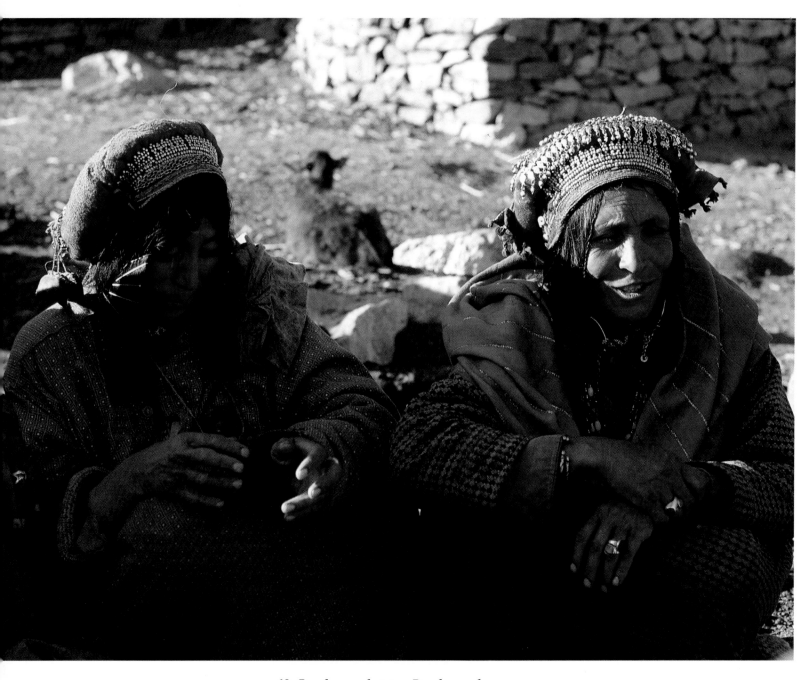

68. Brother and sister, Dozdar and
Rubab, spend the summer in carefree
play, watched over by their grandparents
while pasturing sheep and cattle in Azad
Kashmir.

69. Milking finished, supper prepared,
the women have a little time to gossip in
the afternoon sun on the Tap Alp pasture
at the foot of Nanga Parbat.

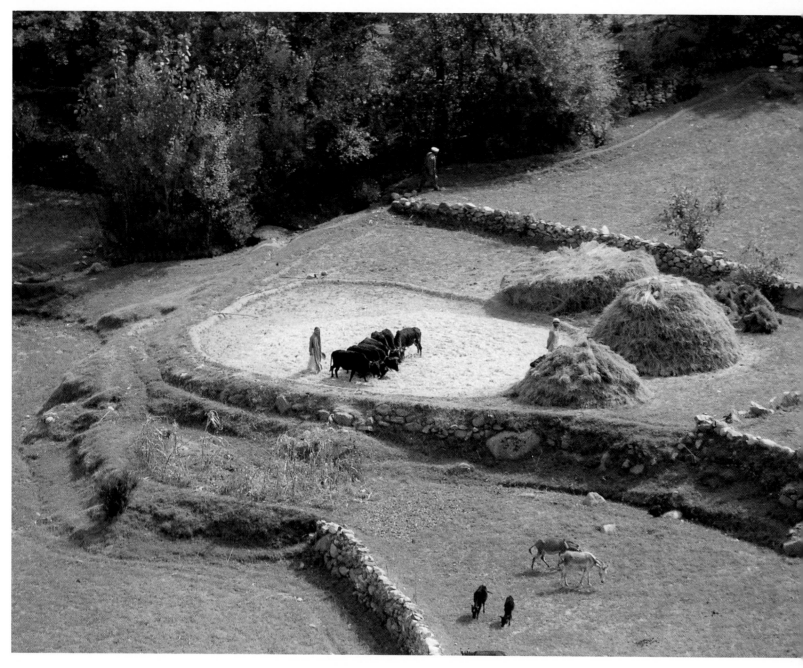

*70. An age-old rural scene: cattle
threshing grain on the threshing-floor.*

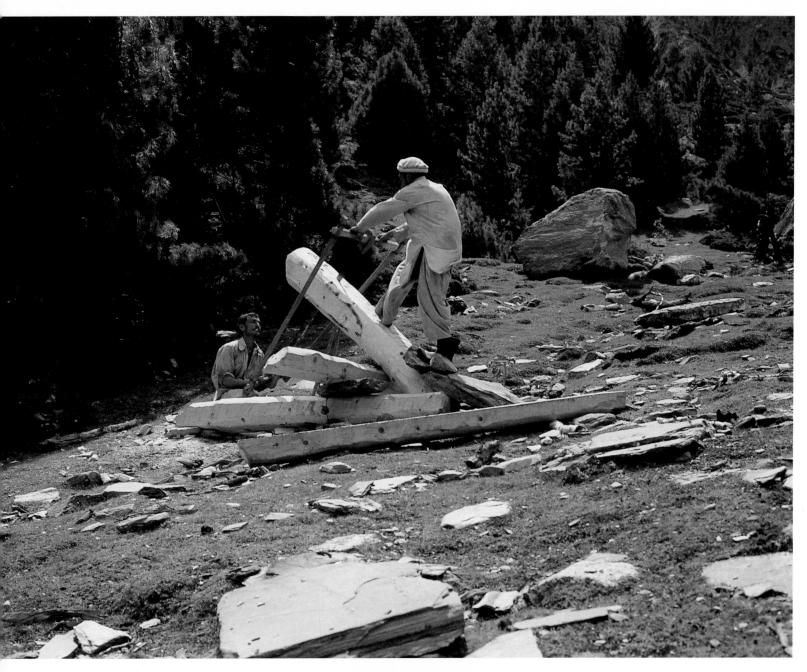

71. Cutting planks with a bucksaw for house building in the Rupal Valley.

72. A Kashmiri shepherd washes a sheep before descending with his flock to the valley.

73. Older children are expected to take care of their younger brothers and sisters. The cloth head-dress protects the little one from the sun, while the kohl around his eyes is intended to protect him from evil spirits.

74. Dozdar is spending the summer on the Tap Alp pastures with his grand-parents while his parents stay at home working in the fields.

75. *Kashmiri shepherds with their flock on the pastures above Sonamarg ('meadow of gold'), encircled by the imposing snow-capped mountains of the Kolahoi massif.*

76. Temporary summer huts of shepherds above Sonamarg. These are 'locals' who prefer to settle for the summer on grazing close to their homes in the valley.

77. Srinagar, capital of the Indian state of Jammu and Kashmir, is famous for its canals, houseboats and Mogul gardens. The city has long been a centre of the arts and learning, hence its name: 'sri' means beauty or wealth of knowledge, and 'nagar', city. It was founded by the great Buddhist emperor, Ashoka, in 250 B.C. The houses of the old city are clustered along the River Jhelum.

78. Houseboats, now one of the
attractions of Kashmir, were introduced
by the British in the 1880s to circumvent
a royal edict prohibiting foreigners from
owning land. Today there are almost a
thousand, constructed of pine and lined
with cedar, moored along the shores of
lakes Dal and Nagin and the banks of the
Jhelum.

79. The Mogul emperors called the Kashmir Valley 'Paradise'. In the afterglow of sunset, the Dal and Nagin lakes assume a mysterious, otherworldly beauty that makes this seem no exaggeration.

80. *In the courtyard of a house in the centre of Srinagar, the beams of the rising sun break through the early mist of an autumn day.*

81. *This Kashmiri boy and his grandmother (overleaf) live in a remote hamlet near Sonamarg at the foot of the Zoji La Pass.*

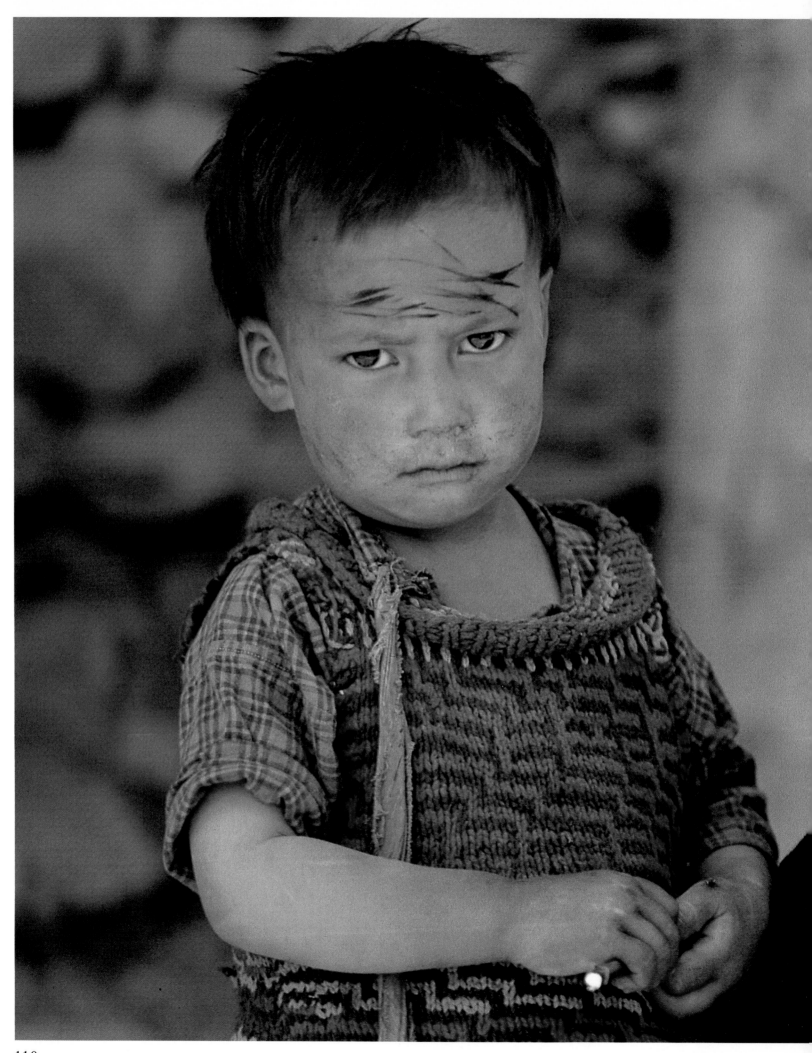

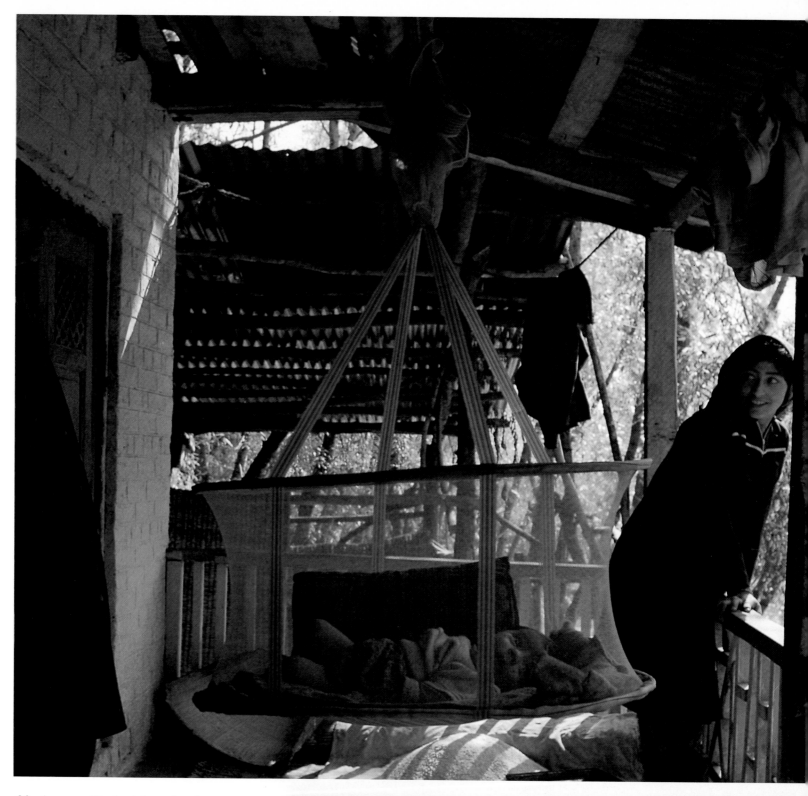

82. *A young Kashmiri mother keeps a watchful eye on her baby suspended from the verandah roof in this highly functional cradle with net sides, which gives him plenty of air, a chance to see and be seen, and safety off the ground.*

83. *One of the handcrafts for which Kashmir is famous is the weaving of carpets made of wool, wool and silk, or pure silk. Most of the weaving is done on hand looms by boys.*

84, 85. Kashmiri shawls, made here for 500 years, are noted for the remarkable fineness of the cream-coloured goat's wool, in fact, the under-fur, known as pashmina, and for the intricate embroidery work. Pashmina wool, which comes from goats that live above 4,000 m, is both very light and extremely warm.

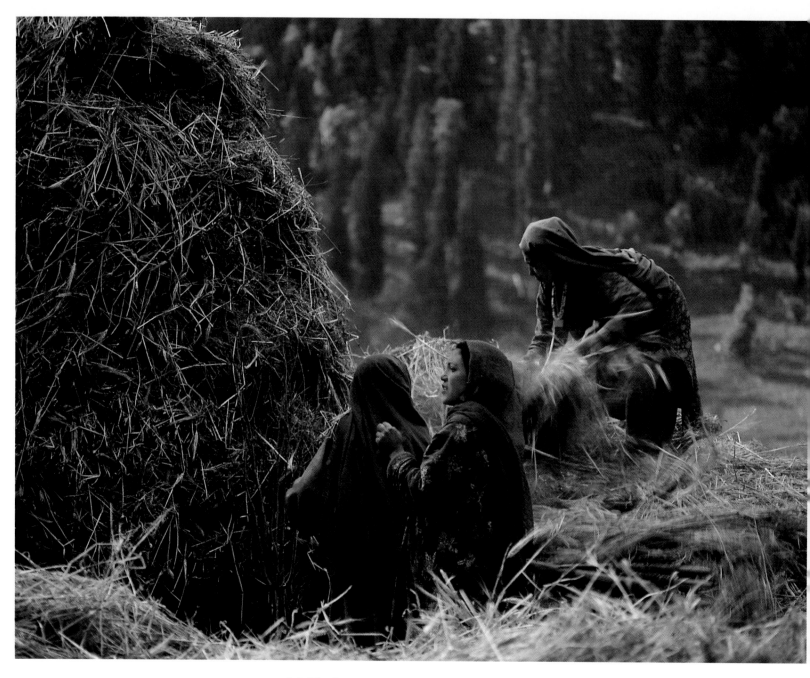

86. *The harvest is gathered, but there is still plenty of work to do before the snowy winter sets in.*

87. Here, the inhabitants of a small village near Sonamarg are busy threshing. Wheat and oats are the main grain crops.

88. The Gujars are one of the few groups to maintain their nomadic tribal identity. Predominantly Muslims, they do not speak Kashmiri (a Dardic language) but a language akin to Punjabi. In summer they live in stone and log huts among the giant deodars near the snowline, in the hills surrounding the Vale of Kashmir.

89. A pretty Gujar girl. Easily identified by their Pathan features, the Gujars are an insular group who rarely adopt local customs and remain socially separate from the Kashmiris.

90. *As winter approaches, the Gujars drive their large herds down to lower altitudes. They are leaving the Sindh Valley in Kashmir, bound for the distant plains of Punjab.*

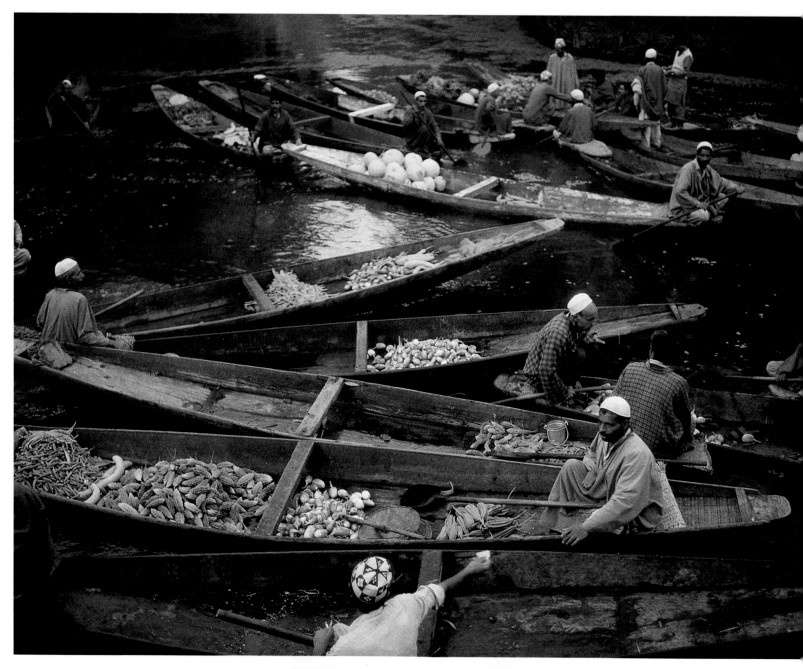

91. Just before dawn, the boat people of Kashmir row across Lake Dal to the vegetable market on the lake. They sit in their 'shikaras' while buying, selling or exchanging vegetable produce grown in the 'floating' gardens.

92. The floating gardens on Lake Dal, are composed of matted vegetation and earth which is cut away from the lake bottom and towed to be moored in a convenient spot. Tomatoes, cucumbers, melons and aubergines grow amazingly well in these gardens. Lake Dal is a maze of intricate waterways and channels among the floating islands.

93. In autumn, the lake is covered with lotus leaves and the canals fill up with tiny plants that turn the surface into a green carpet.

94, 95. The removal of weeds from the lake serves a dual purpose: the lake waterways are kept clear and the weeds are rotted until they form an excellent compost for the gardens. The lakes of Nagin ('jewel in the ring') and Dal are at their most beautiful when the lotus is in bloom in July and August.

Om Mani Padmi Hum. One of the most familiar symbols associated with Buddhism is the Tibetan prayer wheel. Resembling a stick surmounted by a hollow metal cylinder—with a short chain and weight so that the cylinder can rotate always clockwise as a mark of respect for the Buddha—the wheel contains 12 pages with 41 lines of text, each with the prayer formula *Om mani padmi hum* written 60 times, making a total of 29,520 transcriptions. Every rotation equals a recitation of the contents, so that by rotating the prayer wheel 120 times a minute, a staggering 3,542,000 prayers can be sent heavenwards every sixty seconds. As an outstandingly efficient, portable, low-technology message sender, the hand-held prayer wheel has no equal in the world. In Tibet, scaled-up versions, which can reach man-size, are connected to waterfalls or rivers, where they generate prayers without end.

Om mani padmi hum is a devotional prayer and aid to meditation. *Om* is the Brahmin mystical equivalent for the deity, *mani padmi* means the jewel in the lotus, and *hum*—amen. This mantra is popular among both Hindus and Buddhists, but especially among the latter in Tibet, Ladakh and Nepal, where these are the first words taught a child and the last to be uttered by the dying. Simple as it may seem, there are layers of meaning between the first syllable, signifying enlightenment, and the last, indicating fulfilment. The jewel in the lotus has connotations with the lingam and the yoni or sexual act, and takes on a profound symbolism.

The prayer derives from a monastery in Tibet devoted to the Milarepan Tantric school of Buddhism. Milarepa (A.D. 1040-1123), the most popular of Tibetan ascetic monks, was a sinner in his youth, but later began to drive out the pagan Bon faith and establish, in its place, Lamaist Buddhism. He is often seen in religious paintings seated upon Mount Kailas or, like many Buddhist saints, upon a lotus. The talisman of the lotus (Sanskrit: *padmi*) embraces the goddess Lakshmi, Vishnu's wife, who dwells in the lotus. In the classical Greek myth, Lotis, a daughter of Neptune, when fleeing from Priapus was changed into a tree named lotus after her. Homeric legend describes people who, after eating the flower, forget their past and lose all desire to return home (the subject of one of Tennyson's finest poems, *The Lotus-Eaters*). The lotus tree, according to the Prophet Mohammed, stands in the seventh heaven on the right hand of the throne of God.

Widespread as the lore of the lotus may be, nowhere has it assumed more sacred implications than in Buddhist and Hindu art and prayer. Often the flower is depicted as a pedestal for holy figures, as much a sign of spiritual purity as the halo. But the lotus is something more. Quite apart from the elemental parallel with the origin of mankind from water—lotus-like—there is the blossom as a symbol of the vagina and of the rapture of two lovers becoming fundamentally one when imbued with human as well as divine bliss, life and fertility. All of which may go some way towards explaining why such a venerable mantra, composed in a remote Himalayan monastery, has probably been repeated more than any other four words in human history.

Christian Parallels. Although the founding of Buddhism south of the Himalayas and its subsequent influential transmission is well known, less celebrated is Buddhist influence in the West, in particular upon Christianity, which Buddhism predates by four centuries and with which

96. A girl whose home address must be one of the most romantic in the world: a floating garden on Lake Dal.

it shows intriguing affinities. Clement of Alexandria (A.D. 150-218), who repeatedly refers to Buddhists in Alexandria, was the first Greek writer to mention Buddha by name. He knew that Indians believed in transmigration, worshipped a kind of pyramid (stupa) beneath which the remains of a spiritual leader were buried, and practised vegetarianism and non-violence. In Buddhist literature there are many points of similarity with Christian parables and miracles. There is the story of a pious disciple who walks on water but begins to sink when his ecstasy subsides. In another story the Buddha feeds a crowd of five hundred with a single cake from his begging-bowl, and so much is left over after all have eaten that bowls full of fragments have to be thrown away. Another parable strongly resembles that of the Prodigal Son. An early medieval story of immense popularity, *Barlaam and Josephat*, is plainly an account of the Buddha's youth adapted for a Christian saint. One part of the story, concerning three caskets, was used by Shakespeare in *The Merchant of Venice*.

Festivals and Pilgrimage

There can be few places where religious ceremonies are as inventive or as frequent as they are in the Himalayas. Celebration can be simple worship at a household shrine, involve a visit by a priest to the house, walking to a nearby temple, or a pilgrimage lasting days if not weeks. In Nepal, for example, there are one hundred and twenty days dedicated to holy observances involving gods and goddesses, fiends, ogres and all restless spirits. Seasons must be honoured with appropriate rites as well as the personal occasions such as birth, coming of age, marriage and death. The essential purposes of worship are the placation of gods, attainment of merit and removal of sin. The rituals, in the main, involve feasting, fasting, bathing, pilgrimage, offerings, alms, meditation and prayer. Islam and Christianity brought the worship of a single god to the Himalayas, whereas Hinduism and, to some extent, Buddhism celebrate deities native to the mountains, rivers and valleys.

One memorable scene of pilgrimage remains in my mind from a family holiday in Kashmir. From our chalet standing among casuarina, bauhinia and jacaranda on a densely wooded hillside, the view overlooked a riotous, boulder-scattered torrent transformed by sunlight into a mosaic of crushed glass, the colours of silver and bronze; at bedtime it became an incessant and possessed braggart. Across the river, a lush water-meadow gave way to well-thicketed woods populated by flocks of bright, noisy birds. The woods, in turn, merged upwards with outcrops of slate topped by quite serious cinnamon foothills.

One morning our younger daughter, awakened early by children scaring birds feeding among the apricot trees, brought the family smartly from their beds to the verandah with a cry of: 'Quick, quick, come and see the wolf.' Thin, mangy and apprehensively snuffling, only the wild, topaz-eyed gaze and its silence distinguished the animal from any flea-ridden mongrel to be found dozing along the shadier stretches of dirt roads in every local village. We reckoned thirst had brought the wolf down to the pasture opposite. Interest spanning the river was mutual until the emaciated beast, no longer curious, sniffed the early morning air and sauntered stiffly back into the tree-line. Relieved as I was to see the animal depart, even one so dejected and plainly in need of a veterinarian as 'ours', the collective judgement over breakfast later resolved that being brought up by wolves might have suited Mowgli or Romulus and Remus, but our specimen left much to be desired as a foster parent.

At dusk that evening, after a day's pony-trekking that had not been without rather more rotation in the saddle than usual and many keen glances at gun-metal shadows among the shiny greens and browns skirting the woodland tracks, we sat on the same verandah. A spectacle on the facing hillside stilled the habitual family small-talk. Winding their way upwards towards a temple we had visited that morning, a line of thirty to forty thinly-clad pilgrims, their lanterns swinging at knee height, trudged steadfastly upwards. As the last colours drained from the landscape and the figures faded, only the short arcs of the swaying oil-lamps marked their progress, and above the unbroken babble of water came the soft chant of Brahmin-led prayers from the pilgrims. Just occasionally, the indistinct tinkle of finger-held cymbals could be heard, becoming fainter as the devout procession, now no more than a diminishing string of fading, whitish glints, was finally eclipsed by the trees. Younger daughter wondered whether they knew about wolves; I reckoned they did and the wolves kept away from the lanterns.

Unforeseen as it was unembellished, the scene that evening characterised the simply-organised seasonal event or religious festival to be found throughout the Himalayas. At the other extravagant extreme is the Kumbh-Mela, when millions of pilgrims gather for the largest religious ceremony on earth at Hardwar (Door of Hari, or Vishnu). In between is a range of religious celebrations invariably linked with the placation of the gods, as well as a prayer for health and prosperity. All the peoples of the Indo-Gangetic plain as well as those living in the mountains have a reverential snow-ward orientation. Whereas Muslims in the west look further west towards Mecca, for Hindus and Buddhists the way to salvation is upwards. The informal gathering of holy men at a *mela* (festival) provides a forum where views on Hindu doctrine and reform can be discussed, since the faith has no central assembly to rule on such matters. Festivals in the Himalayas, like festivals everywhere, may honour a deity hallowed by time, but the opportunity is taken by merchants to open stalls and sell urban luxuries, women's clothes, jewellery, food, herbal medicines, and the trinkets and toys children gaze upon in wide-eyed fascination. For miles around, village women save for the occasion, plan their purchases, rehearse how the haggling over prices might proceed, and anticipate the triumph with which they will return to their own community.

For Hindus and Buddhists there is no weekly day of rest which is sacred, as Friday is to Muslims and Sunday to Christians. It is the festivals and pilgrimage which provide a break from daily toil. For the devout there is the acquisition of merit—even salvation—and the recognition from friends and family that comes with undertaking strenuous journeys. A common form of pilgrimage is to the Ganges—especially at Hardwar or higher up in the mountains—to fetch water in which the image of a deity might be bathed. From some temples, water can be obtained in vessels that bear the seal of the officiating priests, a popular memento with which to return to one's village.

Diet changes radically for hill-people at festival time. Whereas every-day meals are based on ingredients such as wheat flour, roasted barley, rice, lentils, eggs, honey, a few vegetables, mostly of the squash and pumpkin type, along with milk and milk derivatives such as buttermilk, yoghurt and ghee (clarified butter), for festivals there would be a greater variety of produce, for both consumption and thanks-offering. Potatoes, onions, garlic and green vegetables appear in the marketplace, as well as raisins, almonds, sugar, cashew nuts, nutmegs, walnuts, coriander, cardamoms, ground ginger, dried mango, pickles and chutney. 'Cooling seeds', such as melon, cucumber, poppy and sunflower, will be on sale. Flower garlands, offerings made from leaves, marigolds, red powder, henna, sandalwood paste and cotton threads soaked in ghee, can be obtained from men sitting cross-legged beside the various shrines.

Kumbh-Mela. The Kumbh-Mela is the greatest of all Hindu pilgrimage festivals. Hardwar is one of the four places—-the others are Nasik, Ujjain and Prayag (once Allahabad)—-where the ceremony is held at intervals of three years. Every twelfth year, the planet Jupiter being in Aquarius and the sun entering Aries, millions of pilgrims, yogis, ascetics and sadhus appear at Hardwar on the Ganges. The holy river is said to have first appeared on the first day of the Hindu month of Baisakh or Vaisakh (April-May); bathing in it is an act of great merit, cleansing both the body and the soul. Posies of flowers on a leaf shaped like a boat and tiny clay pots containing oil and a wick can be bought and set afloat on the river.

The logistics surrounding the accommodation, movement, feeding, lighting, sanitation and rotation of pilgrims when millions are involved taxes the organisers to the limit. Everywhere there is the spectacle of priests engaged in holy ritual, naked ash-coated holy men (*sadhus*), legions of pilgrims seeking purification, the police trying to maintain order. The ringing of temple bells and the smell of incense enhance the omnipresent sensation of ancient sanctity. Huge processions constantly pass the two and a half miles between the temple of Daksheshwara and the bathing ghat beside the river. Tamerlane, who was born in 1336 in Kesh, some fifty miles south of Samarkand, entered Hardwar in January 1399 and with the ruthless efficiency for which the Mongols were notorious, sacked the place. The festival survived, and in 1760 became the bloody scene of a battle between rival Hindu sects, disputing whether the Ganges' origins were in the locks of Shiva's hair or the toe of Vishnu's foot.

In the *Puranas*, the explanation for Kumbh-Mela is that the gods and demons fought over a pot of nectar or honey that promised immortality. Drops of the magical elixir fell on four earthly sites, which became the four sacred locations of the festival. Vishnu appeared in disguise and managed to rescue the honey, which was then shared among the gods.

Hardwar's name is a matter of dispute: followers of Vishnu assert the spelling should be Hari-Dwar, (Hari means Vishnu), whilst the followers of Shiva (Hara) insist upon Hara-Dwar. Though it lies south of the Siwalik foothills and is not part of the Himalayas, it is the gateway to northern Uttar Pradesh, through which the holy Ganges pours out onto the plains. Beyond Hardwar to the north is the 'Holiest of Holies' (Uttarakhand), studded with the four sacred temples of Yamunotri,

Paramatman ('Supreme Self' or 'World Soul'), a form of Vishna holding a shell, disc, lotus and mace.

Gangotri, Kedarnath and Badrinath. Apart from the headwaters of the Ganges, the region is intersected by other rivers: the Mahakali, which marks India's boundary with Nepal; the Sutlej, dividing Tibet from India; and the Yamuna, Bhagirathi, Alakananda and Mandakiri, all draining south to water the northern plains. Well to the east is the towering Nanda Devi (25,645 ft, 7,817 m.), which intriguingly, given the number of Hindu texts that revere the area, is not accorded the eminence its altitude commands. The fact that there are over a hundred peaks reaching above 20,000 ft (6,000 m.) may have made the ancient chroniclers blasé and, as in any country, rivers are a far more practical source of well-being for the majority and therefore more obviously worthy of reverence. How reverent is illustrated by the tally of pilgrims who attended the 1966 Kumbh-Mela in Prayag. Fifteen million arrived between January 7 and February 18; seven million bathed in one day.

Badrinath. High up near the Chinese border at 10,300 ft (3,140 m.) and set among breathtaking gorges, Badrinath is the most visited of all temple sites. The shrine has a history going back over two thousand years and the whole valley is dedicated to meditation. After bathing in rock-pools which cool water from nearby hot-springs, devotees ring a brass bell on entering the temple courtyard to attract attention to their prayers. All around are reflecting and alms-seeking sadhus, willing to pass on the distillation of their years of thought, discussion and prayer to those seeking enlightenment.

About 100 miles (160 km.) to the south is Rishikesh, where the Beatles made their celebrated visit to the *ashram* (place of spiritual awareness) of Guru Maharishi Mahesh Yogi, who did so much to popularise practices such as transcendental meditation in the West, propagating awareness of the ancient oriental attitudes to man's predicament, and reaping financial rewards commensurate with the spiritual thirst.

All along the winding Alakananda Valley which leads to Badrinath, the road twists and turns so that sheer cliffs soar above at one moment and steep ravines plummet to the valley's bed the next. The region is inhabited by Bhotias, a semi-nomadic people of mixed Indo-Tibetan stock who are inclined to Lamaist Buddhism. In winter they descend into the valleys, in late spring the men take their flocks of goats, sheep and yak up to better summer pastures.

Hemis Festival. The Hemis festival is held at Ladakh, 20 miles from Leh, at the seventeenth-century monastery which is the home of 300 lamas. In June the monks celebrate the birthday of their founder, Guru Padma Sambhara, with ritual plays in which they wear heavily brocaded costumes and ferocious masks as they wheel slowly, feigning that they are driving devils from the valley, to the resonant drone of the elongated Himalayan horns.

Amarnath. About 100 miles from Leh, in Kashmir, is the holy cave at Amarnath which houses an ice lingham nine feet tall. Every year thousands of pilgrims, rich and poor, make their way past the Shesh Nag Lake, often frozen over until June, and on past deodar, blue pine and plane trees to an altitude of 12,729 ft (3,900 m.). On the full moon of Sawan, in July or August, pilgrims flock in procession to the hundred-foot-high cave to make offerings of food, sweets and flowers to what is believed to be a manifestation of Shiva's phallus in stalagmite form.

Tsongkapa Festival. In Tibet, where the Chinese Government determines the days of official celebration, Buddhist festivals depend upon the lunar almanac, which lags about four to six weeks behind the solar calendar. A major festival commemorates the death of Tsongkapa (1357-1419), a great reformer of Tibetan Buddhism and founder of the Gelugpa monastic order (Yellow Hats), whose head is the Dalai Lama. The Festival of Light in November sees the roofs of monasteries ablaze with votive oil lamps, attracting pilgrims to night-time chanting, prayers and meditation. Tsongkapa brought celibacy and a strict code of morality to the Yellow Hat order and introduced the tradition of abbots donning tall conical hats resembling the mitre worn by Christian bishops. As he may have come into contact with the latter at the Mongol court, it is just possible that Tibetan clerical regalia owes something to early Catholic missions in the orient.

Mount Kailas. In the manner that 'all roads lead to Rome', so for thousands of years the area of Mount Kailas has been held sacred by Hindus, Buddhists and followers of Bon, Tibet's indigenous religion. For Hindus it is where Shiva sits in eternal paradise, for Buddhists it is the central peak of the world, whilst as a Bon centre, Mount Kailas is the very soul of the country. Because of the Sino-Indian border dispute, Hindu pilgrims were denied access to the shrine until, after twenty years, in September 1981, the first Indian devotees were permitted to resume their way on foot on what must surely be the most austere and punishing of all earthly pilgrimages.

Holi, Dusshera and Diwali. The three most popular Hindu celebrations are Holi, Dusshera and Diwali. Holi is a spring festival in February or March, dedicated to Krishna and much enjoyed by children. Water, often mixed with coloured powders, is thrown with gusto by the celebrants on one another and on passers-by.

Dusshera or Durga Puja (*puja* = prayers), a nine-day festival in September or October, honours the Hindu goddesses Durga, Lakshmi and Sarasvati, and marks the victory of Rama over the demon-king Ravana. Superbly made figures of the latter, fashioned from wood and paper, up to 20 ft tall, are set alight in spectacular bonfires.

Diwali or Deepvali, in October or November, is the Festival of Light. Lakshmi, the goddess of wealth, flies overhead on the third night of this five-day festival, visiting every home that has been suitably lit and decorated. Her attention ensures prosperity for the coming year. Possibly the most important Hindu festival, it is certainly the most enchanting at night, when it is a rare window-sill or porch that has no welcoming candle or oil-lamp flickering to catch Lakshmi's benevolent attention.

It is not surprising that religious influence in the Himalayas has been persistent and profound, for Himalayan sanctuaries are closer to the heavens than all others. And when Edmund Hillary with Tenzing Norgay stood high on the crest of Mount Everest, the first recorded men to do so, Hillary left behind a small cross, while Tenzing, a devout Buddhist, made a simple offering of biscuits, sweets and chocolate to the gods of Chomolungma (Everest).

EXPLORERS AND INVADERS

'Be it known to Officers and Headmen of the Pharidzong, Kampa, Tin-ki and Shekkar that a party of Sahibs will come to the Sacred Mountain of Chomolungma... you shall render help... We have requested the Sahibs to keep all laws and not to kill Birds and Animals, for the people will feel sorry for this...

'Despatched on the Seventeenth day of the Eleventh month of the Iron Bird Year, under the Great Red Seal of the Holy Rulers of Tibet.'

From a document given to the 1921 Everest Expedition by the Prime Minister of Tibet.

With virtually no hard evidence to go on, questions regarding the first people to explore the mountains: who they were, when and why they went there, are quite simply unanswerable. In the absence of evidence, we can only speculate. Motives for exploration change with a society's needs. Perhaps early man went into the Himalayas looking for game or fertile valleys. Maybe he just felt compelled to find out what went on in that mysterious, forbidding arena where elemental forces, which he identified with spirits, were at work. In a superstitious man, the thunder of the avalanche, the comings and goings of animals, emergence of rivers, seasonal fall of snow, would have aroused a powerful curiosity. If not in search of his gods, early man may have trudged upwards to find the source of his life-giving rivers, and eventually forged a link between the two.

Alexander the Great. Virtually nothing was known in the West about this region until the shadow of that archetypal conquering warrior, Alexander of Macedon (356-323 B.C.), fell across the Hindu Kush. That so much of our knowledge of Alexander should come from Romans rather than Greeks is testimony enough of the awe and admiration he aroused in the Mediterranean world. Equally remarkable confirmation of his lasting fame as a soldier further afield, was the shout of 'Sikander Sahib', with which his Indian troops greeted Colonel James Skinner outside Delhi in 1803. Sikander is the Hindi for Alexander the Great, and so enduring was his fame that one of the greatest leaders of irregular cavalry was linked with him well over two thousand years after Alexander had marched his army westwards and off the subcontinent of India.

The whole of western Himalayan history seems, by and large, to be about invasion, and the pattern was set with the foray of the supreme warlord, Alexander. After defeating Darius, the Persian ruler, on the plains of the upper Tigris, Alexander set off in pursuit. By the time he caught up with the Persian army, Darius had been murdered by his cousin, Bessus, who had proclaimed himself emperor, but had prudently and promptly withdrawn to what is now northern Afghanistan.

97. A sadhu, a Hindu holy man who leads an ascetic life, meditates on the cliffs high above the Bhagirathi River, one of the sources of the Ganges. The river winds its way down the gorge below the temple of Gangotri in the Garhwal Himalaya, as the Indian part of the mountains (in Uttar Pradesh) is known

98. The late afternoon sun breaks through clouds swirling around the Bhagirathi peaks to glitter on the surface of the Gaumukh, the source of the Bhagirathi River (overleaf). This place is sacred to Hindus as the source of the Ganges.

99. A sadhu meditating in front of his tent at Gangotri. Most of these holy men arrive in May and stay until the end of October, when the closing ceremonies are performed at the temple, the pilgrims return home, and it starts to snow. The sadhus then move down to the warmer plains. (pp. 132-3)

100. In Kulu, the Valley of the Gods, the world-famous Dusshera Fair is held on the Dhalpur Maidan, a spacious meadow fringed with deodar. On this occasion, the figures of over 360 gods from all over the valley are brought here to pay obeisance to the principal deity, Sri Raghunathji. The central place of the fair is a colourful tent where the God of Kulu sits in all his glory. (pp. 134-5)

Although manifestly in possession of the empire, Alexander waited only for the main body of his army to catch up before following, leading an estimated 35,000 men towards Kabul and crossing mountain passes reaching 11,500 ft (3,500 m.) en route. Bessus undoubtedly had full confidence that the natural ramparts and moats of the Hindu Kush, coupled with the rarified air, unknown terrain, thick snow, and unexpected avalanches, afforded him every protection. But he fatally underestimated the resolution, frenetic energy, military genius and driving ambition of his adversary. In campaigning weather comparable with that which impeded the winter retreat of both Napoleon and the *Wehrmacht* across the Russian steppes, Alexander drove forward, inspiring his men and equal to every unfamiliar obstacle in his path.

When the Greek army debouched on the winter quarters of Bessus, after six months of pursuit during which they crossed the River Oxus, their quarry was captured, stripped, flogged, and had his nose, ears and, finally, head cut off. Extravagant and purposefully intimidating cruelty, so often a feature of the administration of an outnumbered invader, was as common in the Himalayas as in any other part of the world. Alexander spent almost three years of his brief life warring in the Hindu Kush or its environs, descending into the Punjab in 327 B.C., reaching out as far as Samarkand and founding Alexandria-the-farthest (later Leninabad). Not surprisingly, his Macedonian officers resented his attempt to force them to intermingle and even intermarry with Persians, although Alexander set an example, not a good one as it transpired, by marrying a Persian princess who, along with their son, was killed during the disputes over the spoils of conquest which followed his death.

While planning a voyage by sea around Arabia, Alexander died in Babylon aged thirty-three. Given that he had so swiftly extended the known world (from the European standpoint) by some 2,000 miles (3,200 km.), as far as the western fringes of the Himalayas, it is no wonder the empire he founded should disintegrate so quickly. Without doubt one of the greatest generals of all time, he was also one of the most powerful personalities of antiquity, bequeathing a legend as enduring among those he conquered as it was celebrated by those he led.

Alexander had always been insistent upon his divinity. For example, in 332 B.C., following conquests in Tyre, Gaza and Syria, he entered Egypt unopposed and marched immediately to the oracle of Amon in the oasis of Siwa, where he was acknowledged as the son of Amon-Ra. Since Alexander set such store by his divine status, it is possible the resident gods among the mysterious mountains ungrudgingly made room for such a determined Greek, who, deified in Egypt, crossed Asia Minor, camped in their Himalayan stronghold and carried Hellenic ideals to their outermost limits.

Within a decade or two of Alexander's death, the Greek conquerors lost their taste for living on the fringe of their civilisation and after bargaining for as much treasure as they could carry on a thousand elephants, which were part of the spoils, they left the mighty Indian Maurya dynasty to hold sway over an area extending from the Himalayas to the Hindu Kush and eventually southwards half way down the Indian peninsula.

Ashoka, Beloved of the Gods. Around 273 B.C., Ashoka, grandson

132

101. A detail from the Hindu shrine at Kedarnath (Garhwal, India), one of the holiest sites dedicated to Shiva, who is symbolised by a sacred bull.

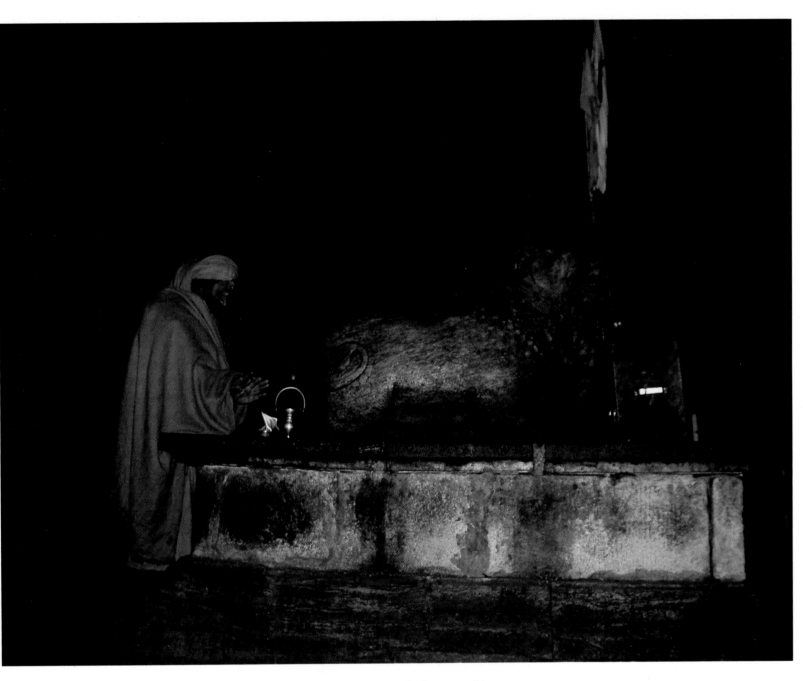

*102. A Hindu devotee lights an oil lamp
at the statue of Nandi, the sacred bull
that guards the entrance to the
Kedarnath temple.*

103. The Dusshera Fair is the scene of brilliant colour and ceremonies, non-stop singing and dancing, buying and selling, throughout the seven days it lasts. It starts on the tenth day after the new moon in October.

*104. The hill-men, the handsome Gaddis,
carry the figures of their gods in
procession, blowing trumpets, beating
drums and dancing. Relatives meet up
here and marriages are arranged.*

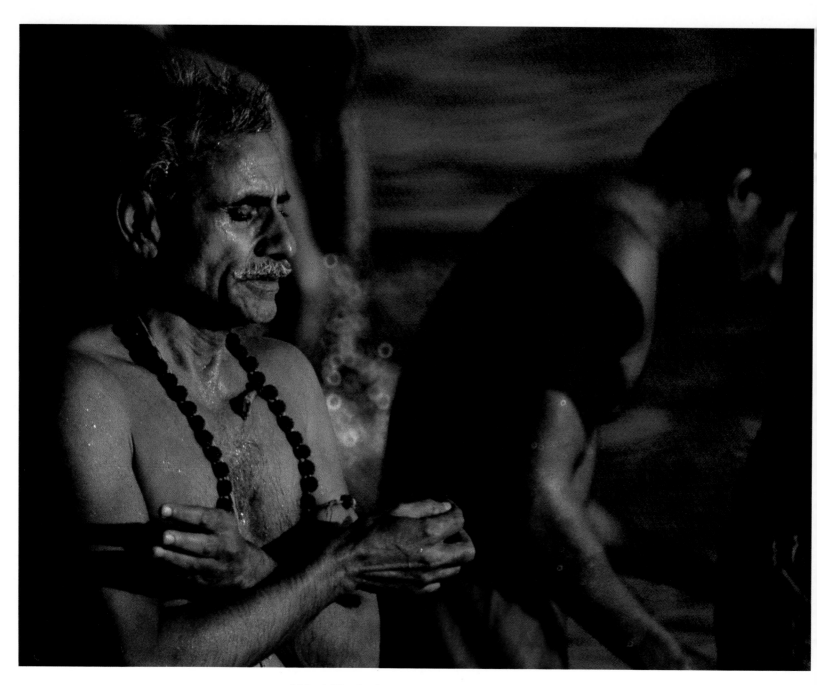

105. *A Hindu devotee making puja (worshipping) in the waters of the Holy Mother Ganges, as the Hindus call their sacred river, at Rishikesh (Uttar Pradesh, India).*

106. *A sedan-chair carried by four local porters is the only means of transport possible for an elderly woman who wishes to visit the pilgrimage site at Kedarnath.*

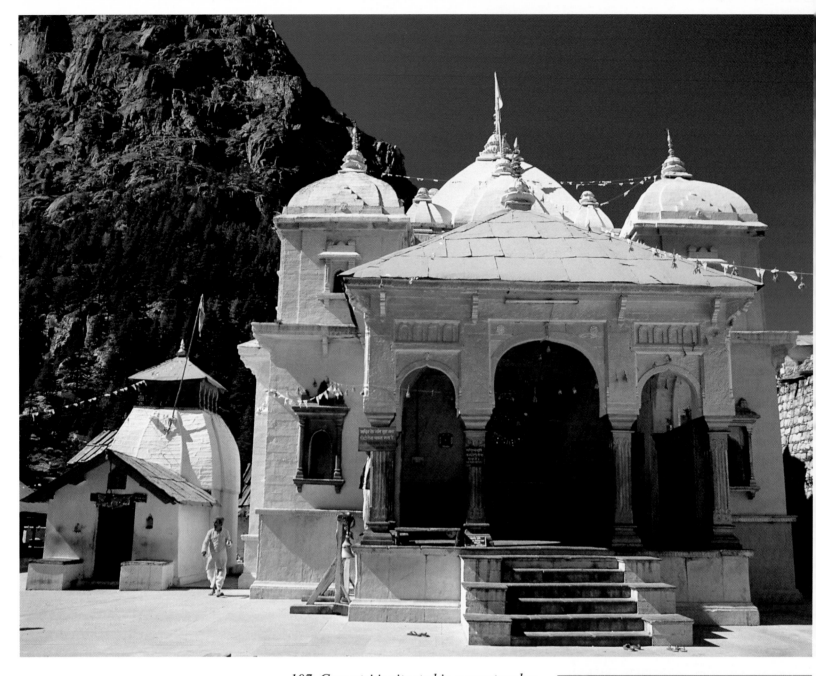

107. Gangotri is situated in a spectacular setting at 3,140 m, in the place where the Kedar gorge meets the Bhagirathi River. Its temple, dedicated to the goddess Ganga Mai (Mother Ganges), was built in the early nineteenth century by Anan Singh Thaypa, a Gurkha commander in the Garhwal.

108. The temple at Kedarnath, at the head of the Mandakini Valley, one of the most important places of pilgrimage.

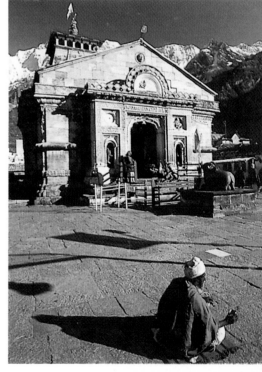

109. The Kedarnath region is characterised by deep valleys, remote gorges and huge glaciers south of the main Himalayas. The impressive peaks of the Kedarnath range dominate the most sacred site in the central part of the Garhwal, recognised as one of the divine resting places of Lord Shiva. The high mountain ridge at the headwaters of the Ganges provides a stunning panorama from the shrine at Kedarnath.

110-112. For young and old, Hindu and Buddhist, religion plays a central role in life in the Himalayas: a Newari girl in Kathmandu; a Ladakhi monk and novices at Thikse Gompa.

of Chandragupta, founder of the Maurya dynasty, was crowned emperor. More is known about Ashoka than might be expected because he issued edicts which were either carved into rock or set upon stone pillars. Like all leaders of the time, Ashoka began with a series of military campaigns, one of which, against Kalinga (Orissa), resulted in the decimation of the population. A rock edict tells us: 'The country of the Kalingas was conquered by King Ashoka, Beloved of the Gods... 150,000 men and animals were carried away captive... 100,000 were killed in action... many times that number perished.'

Some exaggeration may have crept into these figures, but even so, Ashoka, revolted by what he had done, underwent a conversion. Hitherto a Brahmin, he became a lay disciple of Buddhism, and not only adopted the religion but proclaimed his interpretation of it to his people. Four of Ashoka's pillars lay along the route from his capital, Pataliputra (Patna), up into the mountains of Nepal. From the rock edicts, we learn how Ashoka gave up 'tours of pleasure' and substituted 'tours of piety' on which he visited holy persons and places—transforming in the process a breakaway Hindu sect into a world religion.

The two westernmost inscriptions, found at Kandahar in Afghanistan, speak of peace, respect for individuals, justice and non-violence. War as a means of conquest is forbidden; true victory comes from submission to the Laws of Buddhism. The Greek text of the bilingual inscription goes on to explain that the King refrains from killing all living creatures and that hunters and fishermen of the King have given up their occupations. In another edict he rules against violence in sexual relations:

'He who defiles a maiden of equal caste before she has reached maturity shall have his hand cut off or pay a fine of 400 panas; if the maiden dies in consequence, the offender shall be put to death.
'He who defiles a maiden who has attained maturity shall have his middle finger cut off or pay a fine of 200 panas, besides giving adequate compensation to her father.
'No man shall have sexual relations with a woman against her will.'

By far the most famous and loveliest of all the pillars is the Lion Capital of Ashoka, found at Sarnath in 1904. It was at Sarnath that Buddha first preached about the Wheel of the Law. The capital has become the most famous Indian sculpture, being adopted as the symbol of the Republic of India and used on money, stamps, state seals and military badges. Made of highly polished sandstone, four lions sit on a round plinth decorated with four wheels alternating with a lion, an elephant, a bull and a horse.

Although it is enough today to look upon the pillars as, quite simply, outstanding examples of early Indian art, it must be remembered they were constructed for the purpose of political and religious propaganda. Their message survived: the cause of non-violence was effectively espoused by Mahatma Gandhi more than two thousand years later, becoming the mainstay of his campaign to achieve self-government. Nearer to the time of their origin, the edicts on rocks and pillars helped to extend the influence of Buddhism. Ashoka exhorted piety and practised what he proclaimed. In doing so he gave his faith an impetus which literally moved it across mountains and inspired millions of pilgrims to veneration of the shrines, stupas and monasteries where enlightenment and the ministry of the Buddha were to be found.

Chinese Travellers

Fa Hien. Among the first to record his travels across the Himalayas, drawn by the spirituality of the Buddha and the proselytising of Ashoka, was a Chinese Buddhist pilgrim named Fa Hien. His journey, undertaken around A.D. 399-414, took him across the Gobi Desert, through mountain passes into the Punjab and then along the Ganges, from the mouth of which he sailed home via Ceylon and Java. From the writings of this pious explorer it is possible to see how Buddhism was flourishing, respected by kings and peasants alike: 'From the date of Buddha's disappearance from the world, the kings, elders and gentry of the country built shrines for priests to make offerings, and gave them land, houses and gardens with men and bullocks for cultivation... Rooms with beds and mattresses, food and clothes are provided for resident and travelling priests, without fail... The priests occupy themselves with benevolent ministrations, and with chanting liturgies; or they sit in meditation.'

Central to Fa Hien's pilgrimage from China was the acquisition of copies of Buddhist scriptures to take back with him. To his dismay he found that the teachings were transmitted orally and there were no manuscripts he could copy. Rather than return empty-handed, he determined to extend his search southwards, and eventually secured copies from as far south as Ceylon.

Fa Hien is remarkable not only as a dedicated scholar and intrepid traveller but as someone who left behind a record showing that a passage to India from China in the early fourth century A.D. was feasible. Moreover, and most significantly, he ventured so far neither as a warrior nor as a trader; his devout quest which sent him stumbling across endless ice and daunting snow-fields onto hot, khaki plains has all the hallmarks of an exceptional pilgrimage. His precious manuscripts, which he conveyed by sea rather than risk another Himalayan traverse, are lost to history. His own records, however, provide an interesting commentary on Indian Buddhism at the time and the extent to which it drew attention from further east.

Hsuan Tsang. Fa Hien was impressed by the generally peaceable and law-abiding character of those he encountered upon his pilgrimage. The next Chinese Buddhist to cross the mountains and leave a record was Hsuan Tsang (A.D. 600?-664?), who was twice robbed by bandits, nearly sacrificed to the goddess Durga by river pirates, and almost murdered by a guide crossing a frontier. Once he so took the fancy of a ruler that he was unwillingly drafted into his service and on one seven-day trek across the great amphitheatre of inhospitable rock and glaciers, fourteen of his companions froze to death. Between 629 and 645, Hsuan Tsang proceeded from China to Samarkand and then over the Hindu Kush onto the plains.

Like Fa Hien before him, his primary purpose was to see the scholarly centres of India and to collect religious literature and relics. Unlike Fa

Hien, he left behind the first traveller's account of the treacherous terrain, blinding snow-fields and penetrating cold of high-altitude travel in the Himalayas. Whereas Fa Hien confined himself to the spiritual purpose of his mission, Hsuan Tsang fortunately turned aside to describe what he saw. He was also a linguist, learning three languages he would need before he left China, and a diplomat who could take an honoured place at court or in a monastery when in contact with kings and abbots. From his writings we gain a wonderful insight into the prosperity of the peoples he met, from nomadic, fur-clad Mongols living in splendid tents to the densely populated cities such as Benares where, he writes: 'Some cut their hair off, others tie their hair in a knot and go naked... they cover thier bodies with ashes, and by the practice of all sorts of austerities they seek escape from birth and death.'

His is the last glimpse we have of the mountains, the spirituality and artistic accomplishments before the invasions that were to come. Although the purpose of his extraordinary journey was primarily religious, Hsuan Tsang, after his travels from Afghanistan to Benares, retraced his steps to China through the Hindu Kush and Pamirs with many gold and silver statues, as well as 150 relics of the true Buddha and 657 learned books. These were mere trifles, however, compared with the plunder, devoid of any religious purpose, that would follow. Hsuan Tsang wrote a detailed account of his experiences and translated Buddhist scriptures, both of which were supplemented by a biography written by his disciple, Hwui Li. Exploration may have been incidental to the Chinese Buddhist, just as twice crossing the Himalayas was no more than a means to his religious purpose; it is, however, his meticulous observations which single him out as a pilgrim without equal, as well as a man of exceptional learning and literary talent.

Muslim Conquerors

Mahmud of Ghazni. The forces that were to drive peoples from the North Indian plains ever higher into the Himalayas began to gather in Afghanistan around the end of the tenth century. Soon after Mahmud of Ghazni succeeded to his father's imperial throne in 997, he embarked on a series of raids against the politically divided but extremely wealthy North Indian princes, who proved unable to defend their rich possessions. Between 1001 and 1027, Mahmud made seventeen major assaults with a relatively small, but highly mobile army, which desecrated and looted temples and palaces. Enormous caravans of plundered treasure and slaves were sent back to Ghazni, but it was the slaughter of the idol-worshipping priests and populace—-so offensive in the eyes of the devout Muslims—-that drove the terrified people into the mountains. Even there they were not necessarily safe.

Kangra is an ancient town dominating an idyllically beautiful valley of snow-fed streams. Nearby spurs of the Himalayas reach 17,000 ft (5,300 m.) and on their lower slopes vast forests of pine are interspersed with groves of eucalyptus and sugar cane. During Mahmud's fourth invasion in 1008, the town was plundered and the temple sacked. Priests were easily put to the sword, treasure could be transported by slaves and animals, and the large, unwanted, stone idols were smashed. Judging by the state of much Hindu sculpture, later, in the sixteenth century, religious fervour and artillery practice united in desecrating structures so colossal they defied shipment by invaders who, in any case, despised the cults they represented.

For the next four centuries the Himalayas offered some kind of refuge from hostile empires which clashed all around. To the north, Genghis Khan (1167?-1227), after conquering Mongolia and establishing his capital at Karakorum, conducted a series of campaigns, marked by ruthless carnage, from the Adriatic to the Sea of Japan, but mercifully never ventured very far south. Mongol cavalry was better suited to the easier going so graphically described by the Italian friar, Joannes de Plan Carpini, sent by Pope Innocent IV to find out more about the threat pending in Afghanistan and Bokhara. Carpini wrote: 'There are no cities or towns here, just an infertile sandy terrain with no trees but particularly suitable as pasture ground for sheep and cattle. Everyone, including the Emperor and his princes, cooks his own food and fires are made with dung... The climate is far from temperate.'

Tamerlane. This understatement might well have been uttered by the army of Tamerlane (1336-1405), who crossed the Hindu Kush in the spring of 1398, another in the long line of invaders. Experiencing all the rigours known to Alexander the Great seventeen centuries earlier, traversing deep snow in howling winds and dragging military stores up and down rock and ice precipices, Tamerlane's army finally reached Multan in October, and the serious undertaking of yet another pillage of the North Indian plain could begin. It has to be said of Tamerlane, cruel conqueror though he was, that he was hardly less merciless on his army than he was on infidels. Eighty thousand Hindus are said to have been slaughtered at Delhi, and this after a huge ransom had been collected to buy him off. Bands of soldiers raided deep into the foothills, bringing back to Delhi a vast treasure plundered from the temples. By the summer of 1399, Tamerlane had had enough. Samarkand called and, weighed down with a year's accumulated booty, the army made its slow progress back across the Hindu Kush. By this time Tamerlane's thoughts had turned to Damascus and beyond; he was not one to be seduced for long by the luxuries, the gold, silver, jewels, ivory and gorgeous finery he had exacted.

Mogul Empire. Raids into Hindustan continued to bring Muslim invaders from the west into the foothills of the Himalayas until Babur (1480-1530) established a degree of permanency by founding the Mogul Empire in 1526. Nearly nine hundred miles to the south, in Goa, St Francis Xavier (1506-1552) arrived in 1541 to begin his remarkably successful missionary work for the Society of Jesus. Characterised by boundless enthusiasm, invariable kindness, personal magnetism, considerable scholarship and singular common sense, St Francis earned a formidable reputation for the Society, and in 1580 a Jesuit mission was invited to attend the court of the Great Mogul Akbar (1542-1605) in Agra. Whilst Akbar vigorously engaged in continual warfare, enlarging his empire from Afghanistan to Bengal, he also maintained a policy of religious toleration. One of his sons was tutored by a Jesuit and he himself promulgated a composite creed which was monotheistic but included the worship of sun, fire and lights, so as to unite all his subjects in a common belief; it disappeared after his death.

Jesuit Missionaries

The Jesuit missionaries were aware that they were following, by some thousand years, the sixth-century Nestorian Christians who settled on the Indian coast when driven from Iraq and Persia. The Nestorian Church, named after St Nestorius, a fifth-century theologian and Patriarch of Constantinople, opposed the title of Mother of God for the Virgin and lost communion with the rest of Christendom. Its missionaries, however, gained many adherents in the Middle East, India and even China. But more intriguing, for the Jesuits, were reports reaching the mission that there were followers of Jesus, practising rites similar to those of the mission, living deep in the mountains. It is a mark of the successful evangelising of the Jesuits that Akbar himself doubled the sum of 500 seraphins (a small silver coin) provided by the Goa mission to finance an expedition across the Himalayas

Benedict de Goes. This expedition was to be led by Father Benedict de Goes (1562-1607), a native of the Azores, who had served in India for ten years and in 1597 had accompanied Akbar when the Emperor spent a year in Kashmir. No doubt, Akbar's support coupled military, political and geographic interests with religious curiosity.

De Goes set off in January 1603 from Agra for Lahore, and then in mid-summer from Kabul to cross the Pamirs and emerge in Yarkand in November of the same year. He spoke fluent Persian and dressed as a Persian trader whilst travelling with a caravan across 550 miles (800 km.) of the most exhausting terrain on earth. In Yarkand, visited by Marco Polo almost three centuries earlier, de Goes was delayed for a year and then allowed to travel eastwards. More delays followed, culminating in a year spent waiting outside the Great Wall of China. He was still awaiting permission to proceed when he died in April 1607. The priest's records and possessions were taken by those accompanying him, only a few pages of his diary being retrieved by the Jesuit mission in Beijing, which had been established in 1601 and just might have contributed to the rumours of Christians living in Cathay. More probably, Christian visitors were impressed by the similarities of Buddhist worship, of monasteries, a celibate priesthood, solemnly chanted sacraments and the ideal of poverty.

Antonio de Andrade. The legend of Christians in the Himalayas, no matter what its origins, was sufficiently alive twenty years later for another trans-Himalayan expedition to be mounted by Jesuits. Akbar died in 1605, and Jehanghir, his successor, was not as taken with Jesuits as he was with gardens in Kashmir, so there is no record of financial support for Father Antonio de Andrade (1589-1634), who left Agra in March 1624. Unlike de Goes, who travelled far to the west and reached Kabul before crossing the Himalayas, Andrade took the much shorter Hindu pilgrim route, first by way of Hardwar and then on to Srinagar (in Garhwal, not to be confused with Srinagar in Kashmir), following the Alakananda River steadily northwards. Andrade left behind only two brief letters, published in Lisbon in 1626, which describe his journey: '[We went through] snow so deep we sank in it up to our waists... even up to our shoulders. We had hardly camped for the night when we were overtaken by a snowstorm so violent... we could not see one another, even though

Vairochana ('He who is like the Sun'), one of the five transcendent Buddhas, depicted making the gesture of Supreme Wisdom.

we were lying side by side... Our feet became so frozen and swollen that we felt nothing...'

Apart from suffering from snow-blindness, frost-bite and altitude sickness, they were almost lost, being saved by a search party sent out by a local ruler, which escorted them into Tsaparang in the Upper Jhelum valley. Andrade was made very welcome, but found no trace of the practising Christians for whom he was searching. He was, however, told he could found a mission and went back across the mountains with a letter from the local ruler which expressed joy '...in the arrival in our land of Padre Antonio... we take him for a Chief Lama... to be given a site and all the help to build a house of prayer.'

By August 1625, Andrade was back with four others, and in April of the next year, he and his Portuguese assistants had built the first place of Christian worship ever constructed in the Himalayas. The legend which had for so long intrigued and stimulated Jesuit missions in India was now self-fulfilled.

Success was short-lived. In 1630 Andrade was recalled to Goa to head the Jesuit mission; in 1633 war broke out between Tsaparang and Ladakh, which led to the friendly ruler being captured and imprisoned in Leh. Andrade was determined to go back, but died in Goa in 1634. The mission in Tsaparang was suppressed and the city, from being the capital of an ancient dynasty, was destined to crumble into ruins. Founded by the first European to cross the Middle Himalayas, the mission lasted no more than six years after his death. Portuguese ambitions for a mass conversion to Christianity lingered on in the subcontinent, but the epic achievement of Father Antonio de Andrade holds pride of place. His route was retraced by others, notably by Fathers Johann Grueber and Albert d'Orville, who travelled from Beijing to Agra via Lhasa and Nepal. The Austrian and his Belgian companion were probably the first Europeans to visit the Tibetan capital; Father d'Orville died shortly after reaching Agra, but Grueber went on to reach the Vatican in 1663, two years after leaving Beijing.

Ippolito Desideri. The last of the Jesuit explorers was a young Italian from Tuscany. Inspired by Andrade's achievements, Ippolito Desideri (1684-1733) set out from Agra in 1714 and wintered in Kashmir before departing the following spring for Ladakh across the Zoji La Pass, a well-established caravan trail. There Desideri fell in with a Tartar princess, and with her invaluable assistance trekked eastwards through the Kailas region to Lhasa, reaching the Tibetan capital in March 1716, ten months after leaving Kashmir. For five years Desideri lived in and around Lhasa before making his way back to Agra, which he reached in April 1722. He stayed a further five years in India, then returned to Rome to write up an account of his travels and discoveries. His manuscript, completed before his death in 1733, remained tucked away in a Tuscan villa until its publication in 1904 made available this unique account of Tibet and record of his tremendous personal achievement.

In Tibet itself, the amiable reception of the lamas was replaced by the hostility of the Manchu emperors who conquered the country and expelled all missionaries in 1745. Borders were clamped shut and a new mythology began about a Himalayan land forbidden to foreigners and shrouded in secrecy, replacing in the process the old mythology of Christian enclaves frozen in time and tucked away in high-altitude retreats.

Imperial Rivalry

Two thousand years after Alexander the Great's belligerent traverse of the Hindu Kush, the little that was known in the West of the Himalayas was either locked away in Catholic archives or embellished beyond credible recognition. By the turn of the eighteenth and nineteenth centuries, imperial ambition had stirred up political rivalry in the region. France, Holland and Portugal no longer presented a realistic threat to India, or indeed to one another in India, but the three largest empires began to eye each other warily around the Himalayas. Britain and Russia seemed clearly set on a collision course, whilst China's involvement was never to be taken seriously above the level of the minor border officials, who could confidently be counted upon to excel in all the skills of bureaucratic procrastination. Their Government had other priorities. On the other hand, the history of British exploration of the North-West Frontier showed a cheerful willingness to fish in troubled waters, coupled with a justifiable fear of getting too deeply committed. This attitude probably saved the region from being overwhelmed. In fact, tsarist Russia was never seriously intent upon trans-Himalayan expansion, contrary to the view widely held in Calcutta and London.

In the nineteenth century international curiosity was aroused by this complex system of mountains which not only fed major rivers descending to south and south-east Asia and was studded with fertile valleys but also had negotiable passes. Though parts of the Himalayas obviously presented insurmountable obstacles to communication, others could be more easily traversed, so that the pattern of exploration that evolved had a clandestinely military aspect. India had been taken by the sword and would clearly have to be held by it. Anarchy on the Himalayan border would have to be suppressed in order to secure the British Empire's borders and allow trade to flourish. It was against this background and the need to know more about the northern frontier that exploration became a factor in the 'Great Game', a phrase popularised by Rudyard Kipling at the end of a century which had seen Russia annexe territories up to the fringe of the western Himalayas. It was here that most exploration was consequently concentrated, with occasional forays all the way eastwards along its length.

George Bogle. The first of these forays, which set off from Calcutta in 1774, was commercially motivated and testimony to the eternal vigilance and opportunism of the East India Company. The president, Warren Hastings, hearing of a quarrel between rulers in the lands to the north, despatched George Bogle (1746-1781) to explore the possibilities of trade. Bogle's writings reveal him as a most engaging young man, not above dalliance if opportunity offered. He became a friend of the Panchen Lama, dressed in Tibetan clothes, learnt the language, ate the local food, refused to pass judgement on the pervasive squalor, married a Tibetan, and introduced the potato into Tibet. Bogle's best efforts to

113. A Lamaist Buddhist monk in Ladakh at morning prayer, chanting from holy scriptures.

114. Bodhnath (overleaf), not far from Kathmandu, is the largest stupa (Buddhist shrine) in Nepal. Its circular, mandala shape symbolises the universe and the spiritual forces in Buddhism. The square superstructure represents the earth, the cupola above it, water. The 13 steps, leading to enlightenment, end in a ring stylised as an umbrella, which symbolises the element wind. The stupa has four pairs of all-seeing, lotus-shaped eyes, incarnating wisdom.

115. Buddhanilkantha is the only sanctuary that the King of Nepal cannot visit, as he is himself thought to be the incarnation of Vishnu, the great Hindu god known in Nepal as Narayan. The figure reclines on a bed made from the coils of a huge snake, Ananta. Worshippers perform their rituals near the figure, decorating it with flowers and the red pigment of sacrifice. (pp. 156-7)

116. An old Ladakhi Buddhist from Chilling chanting as he twirls a prayer-wheel. (pp. 158-9)

reach Lhasa were significantly frustrated by the Chinese, who were adamant that neither British friendship nor trade was wanted in Tibet. Sixty years later, the East India Company provoked the Opium Wars (1839-1842) and forced trade with the Chinese through Canton, Shanghai and other selected ports —- a merciful providence, no doubt, for the eastern Himalayas. Following Bogle's reconnaissance and reports on the difficulties encountered, Tibet was rejected as a feasible route for the multinational East India Company to pursue expansion. George Bogle never returned to Tibet. Four years after reaching Calcutta, he died there, like so many of his compatriots, of cholera.

As a motive for exploring the Himalayas, Bogle's investigation of possible trade routes had been preceded by searchers for spirituality, conquest, riches, refuge from invaders, adventure, and lost Christian tribes. As the nineteenth century unfolded, pushing back the frontiers of knowledge in the name of science became an additional incentive with immediate appeal. For one thing, science gave a cloak of respectability to the naked gathering of military information. Indeed, on many issues, such as the ability of an area to sustain men and animals, or the seasonal availability of high-altitude passes, the two pursuits were inextricably interwoven. Science, however, provided a moral warrant for exploration, and this was to be reflected in the men who investigated as well as in the books and reports they wrote.

By the mid-1830s, the nature of the threat facing British India was seen as the possibility that combined forces made up of 20,000 Russians and 100,000 Afghans and Persians could advance through Kabul and attack along the River Indus. An equivalent number of British and Indian troops could have been assembled to face them, but it would have necessitated drawing to the frontier every soldier from all over India. Without that threat, there was enough military action in keeping the peace to occupy these forces. Between 1796 and 1820, only 201 officers of the Bengal Army retired to Europe on a pension, while 1,243 were killed or died in service. Too many national interests and empires gathered about the Himalayas for the snow-mantled mountains to retain their time-honoured aura of secrecy much longer, yet the actual exploration was spearheaded by individuals rather than the anticipated armies.

William Moorcroft. To attempt to disentangle patriotism and courage from personal glory or self-promotion in the undertakings of most explorers is, very largely, a waste of time. Obsession is certainly essential, and the life of William Moorcroft (1765-1825) exemplified this trait. Born in Lancashire, he studied medicine in England and veterinary science in France. He returned to London, where he ran a successful practice until, having lost his money in a business enterprise, he obtained a post in India in charge of the East India Company's stud farm. For six years Moorcroft worked with determination and enthusiasm at improving the standards of veterinary care.

In 1812, disguised as a Hindu pilgrim, he set off northwards across the central Himalayas via the Niti Pass, 16,630 ft (5,070 m.), and proceeded west as far as Gartok, where he correctly identified the upper reaches of the Indus. To justify his journey to his employers, Moorcroft confected a plausible story about seeking breeding stock, but in fact came back driving sheep and goats instead of horses. Moorcroft with his com-

117. *Leh Gompa stands high above the palace and overlooks the city of Leh, the capital of Ladakh. The long lines of prayer flags connecting it with the nearby hill are constantly fluttering in the wind, sending up prayers to the gods.*

118. A long mani (prayer) wall decorated with prayer flags at the lower Pisang, Annapurna region, Nepal. Following tradition, an elderly Buddhist passing the wall keeps it to his right. He is making his daily round, twirling the many prayer-wheels on the mani wall, all of them inscribed with the simple prayer: 'Om Mani Padmi Hum' ('Hail to the Jewel in the Lotus').

119. The graceful, marble Hazratbal Mosque ('Majestic Palace') on the western shore of Lake Dal (overleaf) enshrines one of the holiest of Muslim relics—a hair of the Prophet, which is displayed to the faithful on special occasions.

120. *A class of young Muslims attending a lesson on a floating garden on Lake Dal.*

121. *A Muslim Gujar nomad praying near Sonamarg in the Kashmir Valley.*

122. *A Kashmiri woman from one of the floating gardens on Lake Dal (overleaf).*

123. *Muslims now constitute about 90 per cent of the population of the Kashmir Valley. They are mostly of the Sunni sect, with a sprinkling of Shiites. (p. 167)*

panion, Hyder Young Hearsey, an Anglo-Indian soldier-of-fortune, made the first well-documented exploration by a European. The East India Company was not thrilled by his excursion, since there were no horses to show and the two explorers had to be rescued from Gurkhas who held them captive for more than two weeks...

Characteristically undismayed, Moorcroft on his return began to plan a deeper penetration. This time he proposed to cross the mountains and head westwards to Bokhara, where he was confident he would find the elusive bloodstock that would transform the mounts of the Indian Cavalry. That, at any rate, was his cover story, and whether or not he was believed, it established a precedent for Himalayan exploration, which so often involved disguise of purpose and/or person.

It took Moorcroft six years to wring grudging permission to make a second journey. He was almost fifty-five when, in October 1819, he set off with a massive caravan of trade goods to cross the Sutlej and winter in the Punjab before crossing the Himalayas into Ladakh. In order to proceed across the Karakorums to Yarkand, he sought Chinese permission. Given the quantity of merchandise he had brought with him and the threat it presented to Chinese and Kashmiri traders, it was a vain hope. He waited three years, occupying himself with mapping passes and recording all he saw. In the end, he accepted the inevitable and trekked to Kashmir, heading for Afghanistan via Peshawar and Kabul. Then, continuing north-west, he crossed the Hindu Kush and five years after setting out, on February 25,1825, entered Bokhara. He had journeyed across the western Himalayas and the Hindu Kush, mapped and measured his route, held together his caravan through all the tribulations, negotiated safe-conduct when confronted by brigands, crossed ravines and rivers, dodged avalanches, endured dysentery, and mixed in the political conspiracies of the border. And to cap it all, he bought a hundred horses to take back to the stud—-the ostensible purpose of his journey to Turkistan.

Now aged sixty, Moorcroft strung his stable together and began the journey home. It is hard to imagine there was not an Afghan chief along his route who did not feel it would be an affront to his standing if all that horseflesh passed untouched. No doubt mistrust and danger had dogged Moorcroft throughout his travels, which ended in the annihilation of the entire expedition in November 1825. What exactly happened is not known. Given the circumstances in which his expedition met its end, it is no surprise that Moorcroft's narrative was not published until 1841. Moreover, since the account was intended for his paymasters, who were expecting horses, he dwelt on detail and not the daring that took him on 2,000 miles (3,200 km.) of trail finding. Sadly, his account fails to conjure up the courage and excitement of the man and the conditions he faced. It was a media mistake from which many of his successors would learn.

Victor Jacquemont. 'Moorcroft's principal occupation was making love' wrote Victor Jacquemont (1802-1832), an observation likely to be given credence coming from a dashing young Frenchman. It may have been written in admiration or in envy, but certainly they never met. Unlike most other Europeans who ventured into the mountains in this period, Jacquemont appears to have been motivated purely by the desire for scientific knowledge, unalloyed by military or commercial considera-

124. *A Muslim at prayer at sunset on the shore of Lake Dal.*

tions. He was a botanist from the Natural History Museum in Paris who mixed in French society circles and translated easily into Calcutta's. From Calcutta he travelled up country to Simla and then through Kashmir to Baltistan, where he spent four months collecting plants, birds and fish before returning to Simla. The Maharajah of Kashmir found the adventurous young man so engaging, he offered him the post of viceroy with the opportunity to succeed to the throne, an invitation the botanist prudently declined. Unhappily, Jacquemont contracted a fever in Simla and died in Bombay, aged thirty-one. He had played the role of the sophisticated Parisian to the hilt, dining extravagantly, dressing flamboyantly—it is impossible to imagine him disguised as a Hindu pilgrim—and seeming perpetually to enjoy himself. Undeniably the first western botanist in the Himalayas, his diary reads as if he might also have been the first tourist.

The tempo of Himalayan exploration increased rapidly in the third and fourth decades of the nineteenth century, for reasons not at all difficult to perceive. First was the need for military intelligence, further heightened when Russia annexed Samarkand in 1868 and later Bokhara, and to establish advantageous positions along a frontier where possession of a strategic pass could be crucial. There was also a rising public interest in the area which the influential Royal Geographical Society, by sponsorship and the award of medals, did a great deal to promote. To these can be added the arrival in the area of the Great Trigonometric Survey organised by the Survey Department of the East India Company with the patently scientific purpose of mapping and measuring mountain ranges known to exceed 20,000 ft (6,200 m.). In fact, as early as 1808 Dhaulagiri had been estimated to reach above 25,600 ft (8,000 m.), but geographers had been sceptical about such findings.

Godfrey Vigne. In 1835, Godfrey Vigne (1801-1863) sighted Nanga Parbat when he set off northwards for Srinagar in Kashmir on his way to explore the Karakorums, the highest mountain system on earth, searching for a route onto the Tibetan plateau. He estimated the summit of Nanga Parbat to be above 19,000 ft (5,800 m.) when it is actually 26,660 ft (8,124 m.), about the thirteenth highest peak in the world. Vigne spent four years exploring these mountains, and his failure to find a way through satisfied the British strategists that any Russian threat must come from the Hindu Kush and not the formidable Karakorums.

Mountain Warfare

To verify this view as to where the real threat to India's security was likely to materialise, in the year Vigne left India, 1839, the First Afghan War, between British forces and Afghans resisting incorporation in the British Empire, was fought on the Himalayan fringe. British policy and management matched the thoroughly muddled circumstances in which it broke out. Moreover, the unfortunate British commander, General W. Elphinstone, was ageing and unfit. It has been said of him: 'None of his advisers agreed with each other and he agreed with each of them in turn.' A British envoy to the Afghans' camp was treacherously stabbed to death; his severed limbs were paraded in Kabul town, and his body was displayed in the bazaar. In midwinter, with snow a foot deep, after receiving assurance that they could proceed peaceably, the British force of 4,500 fighting men and 12,000 camp followers retreated from Kabul to India. Only one man survived. Hopelessly mishandled as the whole enterprise may have been, militant Afghans left no doubt that they were a force to be reckoned with along this mountain barrier.

Warfare was not always provoked by foreigners. With so many martial tribes in the vicinity, marauding has a predictability even if it lacks much by way of documentation. Sikh power steadily consolidated throughout the eighteenth century: by 1799 Lahore was won from the Afghans by Ranjit Singh (1780-1839), the Sikh ruler; in 1802 it was Amritsar, and by 1820 the one-eyed Lion of the Punjab was militarily well-established in Kashmir as well as the Punjab, and a wary ally of the British. The death of this dominant leader in 1839 and the removal of his firm control may account for an army of Sikhs and Dogras, martial Hindus from Jammu and Kashmir, setting off eastwards into Tibet in 1841.

With so much at stake against the unforgiving Afghans, the traditional enemy, and with the Russians and British intent upon closing the gap between them, to raid Tibet made little sense militarily, although the capture of the source of the wool used for making Kashmiri shawls was the ostensible reason. After initial success the Sikhs ran into a thoroughly awful winter and Tibetans bent upon teaching a lasting lesson to armed foreigners. Of the 6,000 Sikhs who set out, 3,000 were captured and beheaded. Why they were there is difficult to say, but the example of the massacre, coupled with the overwhelming misery of fighting in such hostile terrain, offered a sobering message to anyone else who might think Tibetans could not defend themselves.

The Great Trigonometric Survey

Another invasion, this one with peaceful intentions, now came in sight of the southern ramparts of the Himalayas. Combining romance with rigid scientific discipline, the Great Trigonometric Survey (G.T.S.) began in 1800 in Madras and by the middle of the century had reached the foothills, where it was poised ready to continue northwards on the most difficult and ambitious of its undertakings. Whilst the work of Sir George Everest (1790-1866), a director of the Survey, is forever celebrated and his name commemorated by the highest peak in the world, little is known about the actual surveyors who mapped, fixed geographical locations, measured heights, climbed and explored hazardous ranges, ascertained the sources of great rivers and provided accurate data in easily understood maps.

The basic task of triangulation provides a skeleton of precise geodetic control points upon which all mapping is based. Establishing these control points entailed extraordinarily accurate measurement using a great theodolite which weighed 1,010 lb (458 kg.) and had to be manhandled regularly from one observation point to another. Along with all the camping equipment, the sensitive instruments had to be portered up steep, snow-clad, unknown mountains. Solid stone bases had to be built upon which the theodolite could be mounted. Distances to observation points had to be calculated with total accuracy. Snow could be so deep that a rock base could not be found and the weather, so important to surveying, was quite unpredictable.

Mount Everest provides an example of the time that could elapse between observation and mapping. First measured by a member of the Survey of India staff named Nicholson in 1849-1850, the observations were made 110 miles (176 km.) away to the south and only 220 ft (70 m.) above sea level from stone towers 30 ft (10 m.) high. Initially referred to as Peak II and later Peak XV, it was not until two years after the field survey that it was realised that Peak XV was the highest ever recorded. For four years no decision was made about a name; the policy was to give a local name and none of those suggested was acceptable. Sir George Everest had retired as Director of the Great Trigonometric Survey in 1843, and it was decided in 1856 to honour his great contribution to surveying by naming the mountain after him, though he had neither seen it nor authorised its survey.

Away in the Karakorums, Colonel Godwin-Austen was the first to determine the height of K2 as 28,250 ft (8,611 m.). Although it used sometimes to be referred to as Mount Godwin-Austen, that most dangerous of peaks has retained its cryptic nomenclature. It was not to be scaled until 1954, by the Italian team of Achille Compagnoni and Lino Lacedelli.

About a century before the Italian success, the first Indians to leave their names in the annals of Himalayan exploration began to train for the task of surveying Tibet. It was a time when the western ranges of the Himalayas were perilous and explorers could meet with hostility. There was, for example, the notorious episode in Bokhara when the Emir incarcerated Colonel Charles Stoddart and a putative rescuer, Captain Arthur Connolly, in a pit full of poisonous snakes, ticks and vermin. Stoddart, faced with the choice of being burned alive or accepting Islam, converted and was circumcised, but was later returned to the snakepit. In 1842 they were publicly executed. A year or so after their deaths, the quixotic Dr Joseph Wolff, a tirelessly argumentative son of a German-Jewish rabbi, who adopted Catholicism, later became a Protestant, graduated from Cambridge and was an extravagantly gifted linguist, also entered Bokhara, seeking the release of Stoddart and Connolly. Remarkably, Wolff was allowed to leave and given presents into the bargain.

Meeting a sadistic ruler was one of the risks of exploration. It was, however, a fanatic who assassinated Adolph Schlagintweit in Yarkand in 1857. Along with Herman and Robert, his brothers, he made many daring ascents in the western Himalayas whilst engaged in a magnetic survey for the East India Company. The Bavarian brothers had been pupils of Baron Humboldt, one of the most distinguished European travellers of the age, who had sponsored research into the increase in magnetic intensity between the equator and the poles. Herman and Robert completed their work, leaving to posterity volumes of data but little about themselves. If their courage and dedication have not received the recognition they deserve, it must be kept in mind that 1857 marked the outbreak of the Sepoy Rebellion, when 47 battalions of the Bengal Army mutinied, and within a year the British Government had taken over responsibility for India from the East India Company. Times in India were too desperate for there to be much interest in the Schlagintweit brothers and their distant, tragic, excursion into the unknown mountains.

The Pundits

Exploration of Tibet presented an additional hazard, for a Chinese imperial edict forbade any foreigner to cross the frontier. Moreover, passes into Tibet from India were few enough to be controlled relatively easily, as could the likely route in the direction of Lhasa of any foreigner who managed to get across. The solution to the problem, it was decided by the Surveyor General of India, was to train Indians to undertake exploratory survey in areas where Europeans were unlikely to escape detection.

In 1863, in Dehra Dun, a pretty mountain village housing the headquarters of the Great Trigonometrical Survey, a Captain Montgomerie began training two pundits (schoolmasters). For a year they were instructed in the conventional surveying skills involving the sextant, compass and the means of determining altitude by boiling water. Water boils at 212 degrees Fahrenheit (100 C) at sea level, but at 21,000 ft (6,563 m.) the boiling point is 185 F (85 C) . Less conventional was tuition in taking a precise number of 2,000 paces to the mile and recording them on a rosary which would pass for one worn by any Buddhist or Hindu pilgrim. All the notes of their measurements were kept in a special code and recorded in Tibetan prayer wheels adapted specifically for that purpose.

The Hindu deity Shiva as Nataraja, Lord of the Dance.

Nain Singh. Pundit Nain Singh set off from Dehra Dun in the summer of 1864 and after one or two unsuccessful attempts to enter Tibet dressed as a Ladakhi trader, he joined caravans which eventually brought him to Lhasa in January 1866. By April, he was concerned that his disguise might be seen through and seized the opportunity to join a caravan heading for Ladakh. A few months afterwards he separated from the traders and rejoined Captain Montgomerie in Mussoorie. He had walked 1,580 miles (2,540 km.) and in the process taken the position of Lhasa. On his retirement in 1877 he was awarded the Gold Medal of the Royal Geographical Society for the very special personal qualities he had brought to a thoroughly dangerous and novel survey of a land whose rulers had no wish to be surveyed.

Nain Singh was joined by two cousins when he returned to Tibet in 1867, this time to locate gold-fields and the head-waters of the Indus. Once again he was successful, sending his cousin Kalain Singh to investigate the source of the river while he himself ventured to the bleak 17,000-ft (5,700-m.) plateau where goldminers lived and worked underground, keeping out of the eternal winds that blew chillingly above their heads.

Kinthup Singh. Although other Indian surveyors carried out courageous traverses of the Himalayas, the palm has to go to Kinthup Singh, perhaps the only illiterate amongst the distinguished graduates of the school for surreptitious surveying at Dehra Dun. In 1878, on his first mission into Tibet, Kinthup accompanied an experienced pundit to investigate river systems entering the Brahmaputra. Although the observations were accurate, the measurements owed something to imagination and this was, of course, intolerable in a service which prided itself on the absolute accuracy of its data.

A new leading pundit, a Mongolian lama, was appointed for the next venture up to the headwaters of the Brahmaputra. Kinthup, a strongly built young man, was to act as servant. Although there were indications that the Tsangpo and Brahmaputra rivers were one and the same, there was no proof, and the area where confirmation might be found was the goal for the Mongolian lama and his Sikkimese servant, Kinthup. Their sponsors, who had never shown any lack of imagination, had this time excelled themselves with an ingenious, seemingly simple, ruse. Kinthup was to cut five hundred logs of a standard length, distinctively mark them and throw them into the river. Lower down the river in Assam, other surveyors would keep watch; if marked logs came by, then they had their proof that the Tsangpo and Brahmaputra were the same river. The flaw in the scheme stemmed, as in a good novel, from fundamental differences in the personality of the two leading characters.

In August 1880 they set out for Lhasa and by October had reached their operational area, though there had already been problems, as the lama enjoyed a drink, using the Survey's funds, and was in no hurry. Snow-covered passes and weeks of hard going did not appeal to the lama as much as the charms of the inn-keeper's wife in one of the villages along their route. A four-month delay may indicate the amorousness of the lama and account for the expenditure of every penny of the Survey's funds. Possibly the lama became bored with the lady, the enterprise he had embarked upon, and Kinthup plucking at his sleeve and insisting they move on up river. On a horse he had acquired in exchange for indenturing Kinthup, the lama rode off, taking with him the survey instruments, which might not have been easy to sell. Kinthup, all that remained of the expedition, worked as a slave, escaped, was recaptured, took refuge in a monastery, and eventually made his way to Lhasa, whence he sent a message to his promoters to say that things had not gone according to plan. By this time, he suspected, the watchers lower down the river might have given up, but he would nonetheless carry on with the project. This he did, launching the logs from a deserted stretch of the Tsangpo River. His task completed, Kinthup then returned to the problem of earning money enough to feed himself and tackle the difficult journey home.

Four years after he set out, two of them spent in slavery, the dogged Kinthup reached Darjeeling, to learn that his message from Lhasa had never got through, for those on watch for the logs had long before been withdrawn. It was to take another thirty years before the unity of the two rivers, Brahmaputra and Tsangpo, was proved. Kinthup survived to undertake other missions for the Survey and in 1892 was involved in a reconnaissance of Mount Kanchenjunga. A less than profligate government awarded him 1,000 rupees, and the modest, determined man is thought to have died in Darjeeling shortly afterwards.

Munshi and Munphool. At the other, western end of the Himalayas, away from the adaptations of the prayer wheel, rosary and messages stuck to logs, higher stakes were at risk. By 1868 two pundits had made deep trans-Himalayan penetrations. Munshi had travelled from Jammu to Kashgar and Munphool from Peshawar to Badakshari. In Munshi's estimation, his solo crossing of the Pamirs had taken 55 days, for 25 days of which he was never lower than 15,000 ft (4,687 m.) and for 45 days never lower than 9,000 ft (2,810 m.). Kashgar or Yarkand had always seemed likely staging posts for a Russian invasion. His highly attentive audience learnt from Munshi that Yarkand's altitude was no more than 4,000 ft (1,250 m.) and that the ground from Yarkand to the Pamirs was not a plateau but gently sloping tableland, well provided with pasture. The other pundit, Munphool, confirmed Munshi's findings. To British map-makers and military intelligence alike, the information supplied by the pundits was invaluable. The impression gaining ground was that north of the Karakorum or the Hindu Kush vast armies could be mustered and launched through little known passes across hill-states into the plains of India.

Cold War

Identification of such passes and their possession, or at least some political influence over the tribes that did possess them, became a crucial issue in a, literally, cold war where the realities of geography and climate were often subservient to ambition and the burdens of responsibility. In 1877 the Chinese took advantage of the murder of the ruling despot to return to eastern Turkistan, occupy Kashgar, and rename their old province Sinkiang (Xinjiang), the New Dominion. This forward move brought the three empires closer and did little to diminish tension.

125. Kal Bhairava, God of Horror, a sombre form of the Hindu god Shiva, is represented here in the best-known divine image in Kathmandu. Hundreds of animals are sacrificed at this place every autumn during the nine-day Durga Festival honouring the ten-handed goddess of battle. Durga, wife of Shiva, is the destroyer of decadent beings, but also the generator of new life.

In 1877 and 1895 Anglo-Russian boundary commissions did their best to make sense of areas occupied by fiercely independent tribes who traditionally wanted to rule rather than be ruled over, and lived in a wilderness of ravines, chasms, rock-walls, bleak ridges, shale slopes, drifting snow and turbulent rivers gushing a carnage of boulders and mud. Rivers which promised to provide frontiers often changed course or dried up, whilst tribes frequently straddled rivers and refused to cooperate with cartographers eager to bring order to nature.

Two events in 1895 provide a counterpoint to the time, the place and individuals who gathered there. In the early spring a British garrison was besieged in Chitral, a little known town at the confluence of two rivers south of the Hindu Kush. Over 500 men were trapped by Sher Afzul, an Afghan leading a vastly superior force. An attack on the fort set a tower on fire, but later the British successfully mounted a raid, frustrating an Afghan attempt to blow up the fort with a mine. News of the plight of the British troops was eventually relayed outside, but two relief columns were ambushed when trying to break through in terrain where a few determined Afghans could hold a battalion at bay.

The siege was finally lifted by a scratch detachment of army road-builders working around the base of Nanga Parbat: 400 of them, reinforced with 100 local men and commanded by sixty-year-old Colonel James Kelly. They hauled themselves, their guns and supplies through waist-deep snow, in howling winds, suffering from snow-blindness and altitude exhaustion over a 12,000-ft (3,700-m.) pass and fought two actions before reaching Chitral. Four weeks after he set out, Kelly's epic march ended with the withdrawal of Sher Afzal and the relief of the Chitral garrison.

The siege was raised on April 20, 1895. Three months later, about 170 miles (290 km.) to the north-east, some of the last players of the Great Game met peaceably. Representing Russia were the surveyors who had begun their work in St Petersburg 3,000 miles (4,800 km.) away to the north. Matching their findings were the British surveyors, whose meticulous labours had begun almost a century before in Madras, 2,000 miles (3,200 km.) to the south. For six weeks, in chilling sleet beneath dish-cloth skies, they made co-ordinated calculations which wound up at 20,000 ft (6,100 m.)—well above the snow-line. Remarkably, given all the tension, suspicion and international diplomacy it had taken to bring the teams together, they were in almost total agreement on their findings. By mid-September frontiers had been drawn upon maps, accord reached on all major issues, and after a farewell party the Russians set off north and the British retraced their steps to Kashmir.

Bitter disputes over Kashmir, Aksai Chin and the Russian invasion of Afghanistan would keep border issues alive for another century, whilst less well publicised tribal feuds would continue in their time-honoured manner. Plodding from the centre of the huge Himalayan arena, albeit significantly heading in opposite directions, fewer men than even the modest numbers led by Colonel Kelly had brought science to the mountains. And whilst the surveyors involved may have been no more than signatories to an enterprise begun by greater men, theirs were giant, peaceful, steps for mankind and, in particular, for those living in the western Himalayas.

126. The massive stupa of Bodhnath in the east of the Kathmandu Valley (overleaf). Hundreds of prayer-flags are connected with the upper prayer-wheels on the stupa. Under the stupa's four pairs of guardian eyes, worshippers circle clockwise, spin prayer-wheels and donate prayer-flags.

127. From the Nepal Midlands, the heart of the country, the view opens up towards the Ganesh Himal, overlooking the Kathmandu Valley. (pp. 180-1)

128. Cultivated terraces on a hillside of the Kathmandu Valley. The valley is nearly self-sufficient in grain, for every square foot of arable land is tilled and the soil is extremely fertile. (pp. 182-3)

176

*129. Only Hindus may enter
Pashupatinath on the banks of the holy
river of Bagmathi, one of the most
important shrines consecrated to Shiva
on the subcontinent. The temple complex
consisting of the two-storey main pagoda
with gilded roofs, dozens of shrines, and
innumerable statues, originated in the
first century A.D. Pilgrims from all over
Nepal flock to Pashupatinath for Bala
Chaturdasi and spend the night burning
oil lamps as offerings to gods.*

130. In Marga (November-December), on
the occasion of Bala Chaturdasi, whole
families commemorate their dead in the
Mringasthali Forest above the temple of
Pashupatinath. They follow the
pilgrimage route through the forest,
scattering seeds and sweets so that their
relatives in the next world may reap the
benefit of their offerings. At dawn, they
send the oil lamps down the Bagmati
River and make puja on the ghats.

131. Hanuman, the Monkey God, standing at the entrance to the Royal Palace in Kathmandu, is believed to prevent evil spirits from entering. The statue, dating from 1627, is wrapped in a red cloak and has a thick layer of 'sindur' (red dust mixed with mustard oil) on its face. Every morning, devotees bring him grains of rice, coins and burning incense. Hanuman is a hero of the epic Ramayana who brings success to armies.

132. Temples on Durbar (Palace) Square in Kathmandu, peaceful in the early morning mist.

133. Detail of Mogul architecture: a golden statue of King Siddhi Narsingh, who has been praying for more than 300 years on his pillar on Durbar Square in Patan, just south of Kathmandu, called by the locals Lalitpur ('beautiful city').

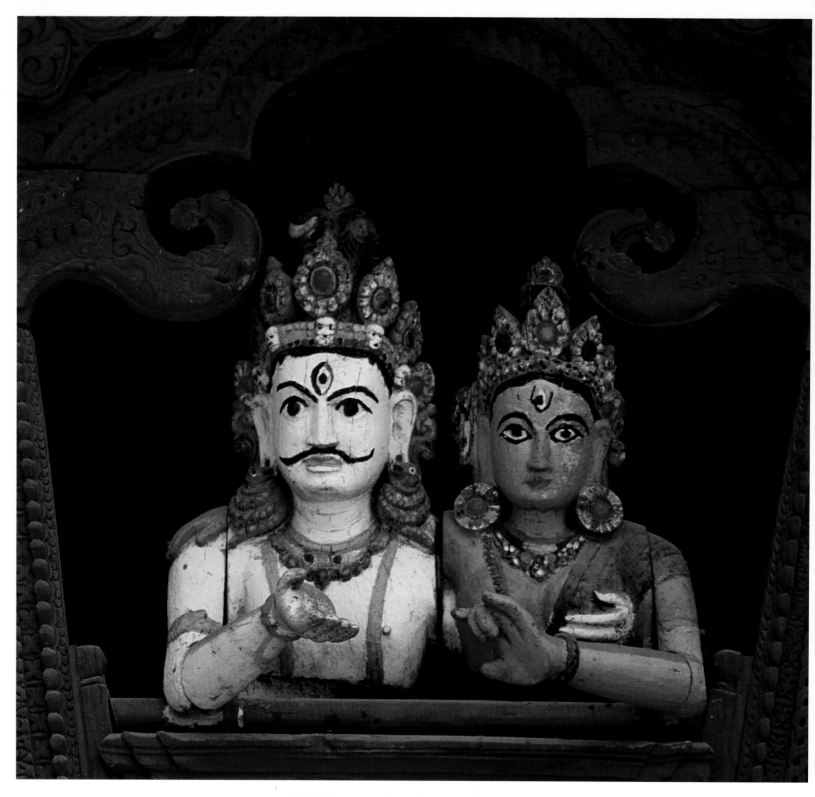

134. Like a royal couple somewhat displeased with their subjects, these Hindu deities gaze out of an aperture in a temple on Durbar Square in Kathmandu.

135. In the early morning the inhabitants of Kathmandu pay their daily respects at the shrines overlooked by Newari homes with delicately carved wooden balconies. The mostly Hindu Newari, predominantly artisans, are an ethnic group, perhaps the oldest in Nepal, numbering about 450,000 and mostly living in the Kathmandu Valley.

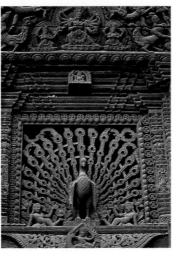

136. A peacock window of the Kumari Bahal, Palace of the Kumari (Living Goddess) in Kathmandu, built in 1757. At about five years of age a girl of the Buddhist Sakya sect is selected as a goddess. She must witness the midnight sacrifice of 108 goats and 108 buffaloes without flinching. She then becomes the Kumari until she reaches puberty or cuts herself. Then a new Kumari is found.

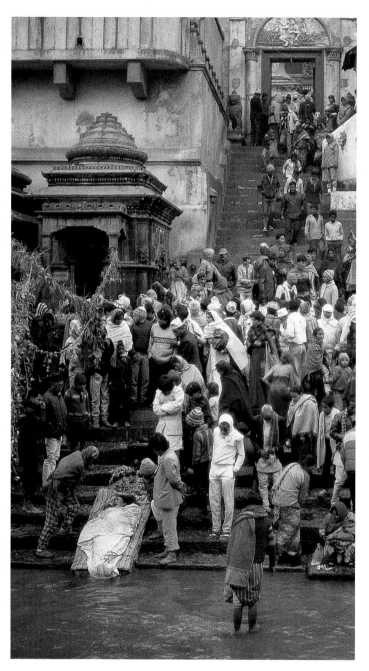

137-140. When death comes, the deceased is borne on a bamboo platform to the banks of the Bagmathi, usually before dawn. At the ghats, sons walk around a parent's corpse three times, carrying the butter lamp that will be placed on the face of the dead person. The corpse is placed on a pyre and the ritual cremation begins.

141. As the priest sets the pyre ablaze, the relatives ritually purify themselves in the river. Then the ashes are scattered on the river and the priest carries the soul of the dead to the abode of Yama, God of Death, where it will merge with the divine.

142. A young Hindu woman. In the nineteenth century, Hinduism underwent a 'reformation', led by Rammohun Roy, influenced by Western rationalism and Muslim practices. This movement improved the lot of women by rejecting many traditional customs, such as suttee and child marriages.

Younghusband. Scope still remained for individual reputations to be made and exploration that was military or political in character continued until, with the advent of mountaineering, the Himalayas became an end in themselves, unconnected with territorial gain. Sir Francis Younghusband (1863-1942) characterises the conversion and perfectly spans the period when change took place. Born into a large and distinguished family with a history of military service in India, Younghusband joined the army but, seemingly bored by conventional soldiering, soon won a reputation as a trans-Himalayan explorer and outstanding player of the Great Game. In 1887, he walked and rode from Beijing to Srinagar, some 4,000 miles (6,400 km.) across unmapped territory, a feat which brought him the well-deserved attention of his superiors. A decade later he was ejected from the Pamirs by the Russians, an action which might have discredited him for being caught. Instead it increased his reputation as a hawkish contestant in border disputes and recommended him as the man to lead an armed diplomatic mission to Lhasa in 1904.

The Tibetans had sealed themselves off from the rest of the world and stonily refused to trade or entertain diplomatic missions. Accompanied by 1,000 troops led by an undistinguished brigadier, 1,500 porters and 7,000 mules, Younghusband advanced over the Himalayas in winter. Turkey and plum pudding were served at Christmas, although the frozen champagne was discovered not to travel well and proved undrinkable. At Gyantse, the invaders encountered Tibetan troops armed with muzzle-loading rifles and charms. Younghusband attempted to avoid a clash, but lamas determined to turn back the mission provoked a battle which swiftly turned into a massacre, leaving 700 Tibetans dead or dying. More one-sided engagements followed, some at altitudes of 19,000 ft (5,800 m.), and in August 1904, Younghusband entered Lhasa.

A convention was signed, peace restored and surveying authorised, but Lord Curzon, the Viceroy of India, came in for a great deal of criticism; popular feeling was that his readiness to move strategic chessmen about freely had gone too far. Younghusband received a knighthood, but the whole episode left a bad taste in the mouth, and because any attempt to defend Younghusband implicated his supporters, few of them were heard. On his last night in Lhasa, Younghusband had a profound religious experience that changed his life. From then on he devoted himself to religious work and to exploration, becoming one of the first to recognise Mount Everest as a peaceful challenge to which all could legitimately respond. He himself made three unsuccessful attempts to climb the mountain and his career distinctively marks the change in attitude that took place.

Other remarkable men would be drawn to the Himalayas: Dr Sven Anders Hedin (1865-1952), the Swedish explorer, conducted three expeditions to Central Asia and Tibet between 1893 and 1908, exploring the sources of the Brahmaputra (Yarlung Tsangpo) and Sutlej rivers and making many geographical and geological discoveries; Sir Aurel Stein (1862-1943), a Hungarian who became a British citizen, carried out archaeological explorations in Central Asia, China and India. More than most, Younghusband, who unexpectedly found a deep personal spirituality, brought away some feeling for the mystery of the mountains, that fascination with the roof of the world that was to replace military, political and scientific considerations as a motive for men to trudge upwards.

143. A Newari girl carrying her little brother stops to gaze at a shrine in Durbar Square, Kathmandu. The Newari, the economically and culturally dominant people of the Kathmandu Valley, have their own script and language (Tibetan-Burmese), spoken by four per cent of Nepal's population.

THE MOUNTAINS AND THE CLIMBERS

'Many times I think of that morning at Camp Nine. We had spent the night there, Hillary and I, in our little tent at almost 28,000 ft, which is the highest men have ever slept... The sky is clear and still... As we strap on our oxygen tanks, I think back to the boy who had never heard of oxygen yet looked up to the mountain and dreamed... We began to climb.'

Man of Everest
Autobiography of Sherpa Norgay Tenzing

The Book of Genesis, Chapter 7, Verse 20, tells us: 'Fifteen cubits upward did the waters prevail; and the mountains were covered.' Which makes Noah's ascent of a high peak the earliest ever recorded and, uniquely, one undertaken by boat. Mount Ararat, 16,916 ft (5,286 m.), would not have been threatened by a 15-cubit rise in water level (a cubit, the length of a forearm = 17-21 inches), but people living on a plain would be endangered, and a mountain top is the likeliest place of refuge. As anyone familiar with mountains knows, the view that sanctuary exists on mountain peaks is one to be disabused. Quite apart from the effects of altitude, and the ruggedness of the terrain, there are dangerous phenomena such as a white-out, when falling snow and descending clouds can eerily blend the snowscape and sky so that all awareness of the horizon is lost. Every familiar landmark is blotted out, nothing exists beyond a few yards, sounds are distorted, becoming useless as a means of judging distance, and with the disorientation comes an acute realisation of the hazards of blundering into snow-drifts or slipping over an edge. Mountains have always been treated with respect, and Mount Ararat was unlikely to have been climbed before 1829.

High passes in the Himalayas, at altitudes equal to Mount Ararat, were established of necessity long before the latter was scaled. However, a radical change of attitude is marked by the arrival of William Woodman Graham in spring 1883, when with two Swiss guides he climbed in the Sikkim Himalaya for 'sport and adventure'. With one guide, Joseph Imboden of Zermatt, Graham climbed an unnamed peak of 20,000 ft (6,100 m.). When Imboden later succumbed to jungle fever and was repatriated to Switzerland, Graham moved on to Kumaon in July and attempted, unsuccessfully, to scale Nanda Devi, 25,643 ft (7,816 m.). He found a way up Dunagiri, 22,828 ft (7,134 m.), but was forced down by bad weather only a few hundred feet short of the peak. He claimed to have climbed Changabang, 22,520 ft (7,037 m.), before returning to Sikkim in October and climbing Kabru, 24,076 ft (7,343 m.). Later, his claims were studied by experts and doubt was thrown not so much upon his integrity as upon his skill as a map-reader. Of infinitely more importance than his accuracy—he was, after all, looking for sport and adventure—was the enthusiasm he generated among fellow alpinists and the interest he aroused among scientists. Graham had beaten a path from the Alps to the Himalayas many others would follow; he himself is said to have lost his money and emigrated to the U.S.A., where his proven pioneering spirit should have stood him in good stead.

Conway's Expedition. In 1892, the Royal Society and Royal Geographical Society combined to mount the first major expedition from England to explore and climb the Himalayas. Organised by Martin Conway (1856-1937), an art critic, writer and explorer—-he became Lord Conway of Allington in 1931—-the party spent from April to August in the Karakorums mapping, tackling several peaks up to 22,600 ft (7,062 m.) and crossing several passes. Of particular interest was the survey and exploration of the Baltoro, Biafo and Hispar glaciers. It has been estimated that 17 per cent of the Himalayas and 37 per cent of the Karakorums are under glacier ice. The Baltoro, 36 miles (58 km.) in length, the Biafo and Hispar, both about 39 miles (61 km.), are numbered among the longest valley glaciers in the world, and although Godwin-Austen, among others, had written about these rivers of ice in the Karakorums, in the vicinity of K2, it was the Conway expedition that made known their importance. Besides the methodical recording of the physical effects of climbing on the members of the party, another of the benefits was the emergence of Charles Bruce (1866-1939) as one of the great pioneers of Himalayan climbing. Then a lieutenant in the 5th Gurkha Rifles, he went on to become a general and to lead the attempts upon Everest in 1922 and 1924. It was his knowledge of the peoples living in the mountains that led from the employment of Gurkhas to the recruitment of Sherpas as guides, porters and fellow-climbers.

Nanga Parbat. Bruce and two of his Gurkhas joined Albert Mummery (1855-1895), Geoffrey Hastings (1860-1941) and Professor John Collie (1859-1942) to reconnoitre Nanga Parbat, 26,660 ft (8,125 m.), the ninth highest peak in the world, in 1895. When his leave expired, Bruce had to return to his regiment, leaving his two Gurkhas with the experienced Alpine climbers. Professor Collie, an eminent chemist and noted epicure, was made unwell by the dietary rigours of the expedition and he and Hastings, who had gone off to obtain fresh supplies, were not included in the final assault.

Mummery, who had been a sickly child and had poor eyesight, was a leading climber of his day who appeared to need to prove himself. He may have underestimated both the difficulty of the transition from climbing in the Alps to climbing in the Himalayas, as well as the Naked Mountain (the translation of its Sanskrit name). After reaching 20,000 ft (6,660 m.) Mummery judged the summit was within reach and on August 23 set off with the two Gurkhas. They were last seen the next day; no further trace of them was ever found.

The most likely explanation for their disappearance is an avalanche, a frequent occurrence in the area where they were climbing. Although there was no evidence as to the precise nature of the tragedy, there were some lessons to be learnt. The diet, the time required for acclimatisation at altitude, and the validity of Alpine techniques on Himalayan giants were all called into question. Nanga Parbat was not tackled again seriously for thirty-seven years, and it was a further twenty-one years before the summit was reached by the Austrian climber, Herman Buhl, in 1953.

Between 1932 and 1939, Nanga Parbat was the target for five

German expeditions. The second and third of these were among the worst disasters in the history of climbing in the Himalayas. The first team, in 1932, got off to a good start with fine weather, but not enough was understood by the leader about the importance of porters when establishing camps. As a result only three men out of the eight climbers reached 22,800 ft (7,125 m.). The expedition came to be regarded as a successful reconnaissance and the experience gathered of value to the team, which climbed together in 1934.

Nine climbers and 35 Sherpas, of whom about half had experience at altitude, set out in May. There was a set-back in early June when one of the German climbers developed pneumonia and died, but climbing continued and by early July the highest camp was established at 25,280 ft (7,900 m.), with climbers poised for the trek to the summit. Then the wind rose to a howling blizzard and raged among the scattered and not fully stocked bivouacs; communication and the preparation of even the simplest food were impossible. The storm lashed for five days, claiming the lives of three Germans and six Sherpas. From the survivors came tales of heroism, frost-bite, exhaustion, and the horrifying recognition by those above and those below that rescue in such conditions was impossible.

Despite the catastrophe, another team of eight Germans, led by Karl Wien (1906-1937) and accompanied by 12 Sherpas went back to Nanga Parbat in 1937. In mid-June Wien, with six Germans and nine Sherpas, made camp at about 20,300 ft (6,344 m.). One midnight, while they were asleep, a huge avalanche buried the site in snow as much as ten feet deep. All of them perished.

Another German attempt in 1938 introduced the novel idea of an aircraft to drop supplies, to counter the understandable reluctance of experienced Sherpas to climb a mountain so implacably hostile. The weather was unfavourable and after two attempts were frustrated, the leader sensibly decided to bring everyone down off the mountain. In the fateful year of 1939, a German party of four examined alternative routes up Nanga Parbat; when World War II broke out they were interned in India. One of the four was Heinrich Harrer, an Austrian, who, together with the team leader, escaped and made his way to neutral Tibet. There he learnt Tibetan and became a confidant and tutor of the Dalai Lama. His account of those times and record of a trek of 1,000 miles (1,600 km.) which took two years and included crossing the Himalayas was published in 1953 as *Seven Years in Tibet*, and became an international best-seller. In a curious reversal of fate, the Dalai Lama who was tutored by a fugitive became one himself when he fled to India in 1959 to escape Chinese persecution.

Nanga Parbat, 900 miles (1,450 km.) to the north-west of Everest, would stay brooding and unconquered until finally scaled in the same summer of 1953. Three years previously, Tenzing had climbed on the Naked Mountain after the Pakistan Government suddenly withdrew permission for the group he accompanied to climb in the Karakorums because of the presence of Sherpas in the party. No one expected to go high in December, and the two British army officers who led the expedition were last seen at about 18,000 ft (5,500 m.) on the eastern ridge. When they failed to return, Tenzing and others went to look for them, even attempting to pitch a tent on a glacier in winter, '... an experience I would not like to have again. Though we were hardly more than at the foot of Nanga Parbat, it was colder than I have ever known it to be on a mountain.' The temperature went down to 40 below zero. The tent canvas and ropes were as rigid as his mittens and impossible to bend—-as if they were made of iron. To have taken his mittens off, even for a few seconds, would have brought on frost-bite. The two army officers were never found.

When the Germans arrived in Pakistan in spring 1953, they immediately ran into the same problem and seven Indian Sherpas who had been engaged had to return. In their place, 17 local men from Hunza were recruited. There were 10 climbers in the Austro-German party, two of whom, Herman Buhl and Otto Kempter, were poised on July 2 at about 22,780 ft (7,590 m.). Weather reports warned of an imminent monsoon, not too surprising as conditions on the way up had varied between extremes of heavy snowfalls and bright clear skies. These reports were passed up to the climbers by a radio network maintained in the base camp. At 2.30 a.m., Buhl, having failed to waken his companion, exhausted by step-cutting the day before, set off alone by the bright light of the moon. Kempter followed behind by half-an-hour, into a fine dawn and day of dazzling sunshine. He caught sight of Buhl a mile or so ahead, but despite resting Kempter was too fatigued to have any hope of catching up. Wisely, he decided at 25,000 ft (7,812 m.) to turn back and reached camp, where he and his companions spent an anxious night.

Buhl, meanwhile, had continued above a mile-high vertical drop, '...never had I seen such an abyss', fortified by tablets to keep him awake, and at 7 p.m., crawling on his hands and knees, was startled to find he could go no further: the lone Austrian had reached the summit. Thirty-one before him had died in the attempt. He took photographs for ten minutes and then descended a short way to spend seven hours resting against a rock in the bitterly cold night. At 4 a.m. in moonlight he began the descent, staggering downwards with a frost-bitten foot until at 6 p.m. on July 4 he met up with his companions, who were looking for him. Going it alone was to make Buhl the subject of a great deal of criticism. Certainly his action violated the code of team-work; on the other hand, he paid the personal price of frost-bite and brought a triumph to his team merely weeks after Everest was climbed. Only three years later he was killed while descending from Choglisa, 25,148 ft (7,665 m.), in the Karakorums.

Almost a century after Mummery's death, in July 1991 two Britons, Roger Mears and David Walsh, braced themselves in the cold winds above the cloud-wreathed upper slopes of Nanga Parbat, which they had just scaled, using the Alpine style of carrying only what would fit into a rucksack. It was a century which had seen the essentially sporting climbs of individuals give way to national expeditions with scores of porters, oxygen, tons of high-tech apparatus, after which—in the cyclic nature of things—climbing reverted again to individuals. The Himalayas would be scaled by many different nationalities; women would reach the highest peaks; new routes up would be found on mountains already conquered, and novel ways down would add skiing, rafting, hang-gliding and jeep safaris to the more traditional trekking. Clothing became lighter, understanding of the problems improved, tourism popularised the area, and the greatest mountain wall in the world edged fractionally closer to being its

Manjushri, an important bodhisattva in Mahayana Buddhism, who symbolises insight and widom.

197

centre, in the way its earliest admirers and pilgrims had professed.

Kanchenjunga. In August 1905, a combined French, Swiss and British expedition visited Sikkim to climb Kanchenjunga, 28,208ft (8,597 m.). The only British member was Aleister Crowley (1875-1947), the son of a wealthy brewer, later to be known as a bad poet and infamous supporter of Cabbalistic magic. One of the leading diabolists of his time, who believed himself to be the Beast from the Book of Revelation, he would seem the most unlikely person to be selected as a climbing companion. Nonetheless, his credentials as a climber were good. Having begun in his teens, he arrived in Sikkim with experience of difficult ascents in the Alps, in Mexico and upon K2, where his colleagues reached above 21,000 ft (6,562 m.). On September 1, whilst descending from around 20,000 ft (6,250 m.), three Europeans roped together with with three porters slipped on an ice-slope. In the ensuing avalanche, a European and the three porters were killed. Crowley, although nearby in a tent, took no part in the rescue, a sequel less surprising than his selection in the first place. After such a disaster, the attempt on Kanchenjunga was abandoned, as was Crowley's career as a mountaineer.

The name of this mountain means 'Great Snow with Five Treasures'. According to Sherpa Tenzing, these are: salt; gold and turquoise; holy books; weapons; crops and medicine. Lord Hunt, leader of the first successful Everest expedition, thought it presented even greater problems than any other of the major peaks. I remember my own disappointment, on first visiting Darjeeling, when I looked towards it, camera at the ready, only to find that warm air currents had blown upwards about the snow-shrouded peak to engulf the upper half in thick cloud. Kanchenjunga disenchanted many climbers until 1955, when a successful British expedition was led by Dr Charles Evans, a member of the 1953 Everest team. He was later knighted and became Principal of the University College of North Wales.

K2. The gauntlet of national competitive climbing in the Himalayas was thrown down by the Italian expedition of 1909. Under the leadership of the Duke of the Abruzzi (1873-1933), grandson of King Victor Emmanuel II, the party was made up of a physician, a surveyor and a photographer, along with seven Italian guides. The Duke was a remarkable man by any standards. He had climbed with Mummery in the Alps when the latter was regarded as the leading climber of his day. In 1897 he scaled Mount St Elias,18,000 ft (5,625 m.), in Alaska, after a projected expedition to Nanga Parbat was cancelled due to cholera in India. Two years later his attention turned to reaching the North Pole, but frost-bite, which cost him two fingers, compelled him to return to Italy and the expedition under his deputy was forced to retire when within 220 miles (352 km.) of its goal. He climbed in Africa in 1906 and during World War I was appointed commander-in-chief of the Italian Fleet; after the war he was responsible for colonisation in Eritrea, where he died.

For the first two months the Duke's expedition reconnoitred the approaches to K2, 28,250 ft (8,610 m.), arguably the most difficult of the 8,000-m. peaks. They eliminated those routes thought to be unscalable, finally selecting what is known as the Abruzzi Ridge as the most promising. At 22,000 ft (6,875 m.) the Duke abandoned the attempt, finding the going too difficult for his inexperienced Balti porters. Although he went on to make three other advances, he was unable to find a better path and his highest point on K2 was reached on the first assault. Throughout their time on the mountain, the party had been exposed to awful weather, which began to take its inevitable toll of their health. Prudently, the Duke decided that K2 was beyond the reach of his team and decided to move southwards to tackle the Choglisa peak, 25,100 ft (7,843 m.).

By mid-July the expedition was climbing 2,000 ft (625 m.) below the summit and trudging in thick snow, which fell for days. On July 18, the Duke and three companions set out at 5.30 a.m. from a bivouac tent at 22,483 ft (7,025 m.), pushed upwards through watery mist, and by one o'clock had reached 24,600 ft (7,687 m.). Above them a snow slope rose into the ubiquitous grey pall of mist. After waiting two hours in the hope that visibility would improve, the Duke took the reluctant decision to withdraw, for if the sun had not penetrated the fog by the afternoon, it was unlikely to do so. After fourteen and a half hours, at 8 p.m., the Duke and his team rejoined their companions in a driving snowstorm that served to underline the wisdom of retiring. Weather, like health, often has the last say. But the expedition had reached the greatest altitude ever climbed at that date, and it would be more than a decade before anyone went higher. Mapping and photography were completed with precision, and the expedition throughout benefited from the thorough planning and good judgement of its leader, who had, finally, the depressing responsibility of deciding enough was enough when their goal was so close.

K2 was attempted again in 1953, when Dr Charles Houston brought in a very young team of six fellow Americans. By early August they were acclimatised, confident, and well-placed at 25,00 ft (7,800 m.) to go to the summit. Then the weather, which had never been clement, deteriorated, and a member of the team developed blood clots in the leg that subsequently passed to his lung. Every priority was given to getting him down; a precarious enough undertaking in blizzard conditions was made doubly so because the sick man had to be dragged through the snow and lowered by rope down steep faces. There was a slip when five climbers fell and had to be retrieved. Shortly after, the disabled patient, helplessly wrapped in sleeping bags, was swept to his death by an avalanche. It took the survivors three more days in raging storms to reach a lower camp and relative safety. K2 had been unrelenting; it was providential that they did not all share the same fate.

In 1954, Ardito Desio, Professor of Geology at Milan University, led a team of 11 climbers and six scientists, who laboured upwards for five weeks. They, too, had a fatality, through pneumonia, but without their predecessors' dire consequences. On July 28, they were camped on the same site used by the Americans before their tragic descent, and from there managed to send Achille Compagnoni and Lino Lacedelli to the summit. In spite of the failure of their oxygen just below the peak, they reached their goal at the late hour of 6 p.m. Frost-bitten, bruised and tired, they made their way down despite avalanches, tumbles and the increasing cold that came with the dark. Another great peak had been conquered.

Everest, the Early Attempts. Nothing symbolises the sobering might of the Himalayas better than Everest, at 29,028 ft (8,849 m.) the greatest challenge of all mountain giants. Tibetans call it Chomolungma

144. The snow peaks of the high Himalayas are the ultimate challenge for climbers. In the picture: the photographer's wife, Ines.

(Mother Goddess of the Winds), the Nepalese know it as Sagar Matha (Forehead of the Seas), although Tenzing Norgay, who was born and brought up close by, thought of it as 'The Mountain So High No Bird Can Fly Over It' and liked this name best for the peak with which his name will be forever associated.

In the 1930s, international competition—the Berlin Olympics, the land speed record, grand prix racing, the Schneider Trophy—was keen and very often heavily subsidised. Hitler was determined to lift German self-esteem after the disastrous 1914-1918 war and subsequent economic collapse. Mountaineering became one of the tournament arenas, with the Germans concentrating upon Nanga Parbat and Kanchenjunga, the Americans and Italians upon K2, the French upon Annapurna, and the British upon Everest. The Swiss, Austrians, Japanese, Chinese, Indians and many others all competed, and, of course, there were numerous combined expeditions, notably, the Anglo-American group, led by T. Graham Brown (1882-1965), Professor of Physiology at the University of Wales, which successfully climbed Nanda Devi in 1936.

Although Everest is five miles (8 km.) high, height is not the only criterion by which a mountain is judged. Mountaineering is a complex undertaking embracing the place, the people climbing, the conditions, technique and equipment, planning, and the one factor about which there is never any dispute—a fair share of good luck. It is never necessary to think up excuses for failure on a Himalayan climb; the mountains will supply endless reasons and show surprising versatility in devising something new to sustain an enduring respect. Inevitably, the challenge is closely linked to the degree of difficulty, and whilst early climbers sensibly looked for the easiest way to scale a peak, their successors searched for new approaches previously dismissed as too dangerous. Once the major peaks were vanquished, the emphasis switched from getting to the top to the climb itself. That said, there can be no doubt that the great 26,000 ft (8,000 m.) mountains will always be the supreme testing ground. Even today the north face of Broad Peak and the east face of Kanchenjunga are still unclimbed, and of the four hundred or so peaks between 23,000 and 26,000 ft, there remain 170 with crests which have yet to be claimed.

Chosen to lead the first reconnaissance of Everest, in 1921, was Lieutenant-colonel Charles Howard-Bury (1883-1963). Before setting out, he had to obtain permission from the Dalai Lama, as the expedition's approach was to be made through Tibet. To the Sherpas who accompanied the party, it seemed curious to tackle Chomolungma from the north, deviating so far from the direct route; the fact was that leave to enter Tibet had been obtained, whereas no westerners were allowed into Nepal. From mid-May until the end of September, nine British climbers with 40 porters probed and climbed, reaching 23,000 ft (7,187 m.) and, more significantly, found a possible route to the top. George Mallory (1886-1924), a schoolmaster at Charterhouse, reached a point from which he believed an attack might be possible; to his dismay, the wind intensified and the path which he and his companions sought to follow was engulfed in a frightening blizzard. The climbers were tired, the hazards all too obvious, and the primary purpose of reconnaissance had been completed. Prudence dictated a withdrawal and Mallory really had no choice.

145. Annapurna South (7,219 m.), seen from Modi Khola (overleaf). As it stands at the source of the Modi Khola, the peak is also called Moditse ('tse' = mountain).

146. The summit of Thorugtse (6,482 m.) to the north of the Thorong La Pass, at sunset. (pp. 204-5)

147. Behind the tree-fringed ridge rises majestic Annapurna South, seen from Ghandrung. (pp. 206-7)

200

148. *View from the Thorong La Pass (5,416 m.) towards the Chulu peaks in the north-east.*

149. *Seen from the Annapurna base camp: the overwhelming panorama of the south face of Annapurna I (8,091 m.). In Sanskrit, the name means 'goddess of the abundant harvest'.*

150. There is no rest for the local porters. In all weathers they tote their heavy loads through the rhododendron forest from Ghandrung to Ghorapani.

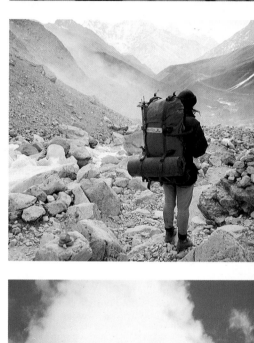

151-160. Climbing in the Himalayas (this page and opposite). Most ascents are made with the help of altitude camps and fixed ropes. Normally three or four tent camps stocked with food and sleeping bags are established on the mountain before an attempt is made to reach the summit.

161-163. The photographer's base camp under Nanga Parbat (far left). The ascent from the valley to the base camp is called the approach march. For this section, expeditions use low-altitude porters, usually local people (left). The serious climbing begins from the base camp. Above, Camp I at an altitude of 5,500 m. on the Kupol face of Nanga Parbat (Pakistan).

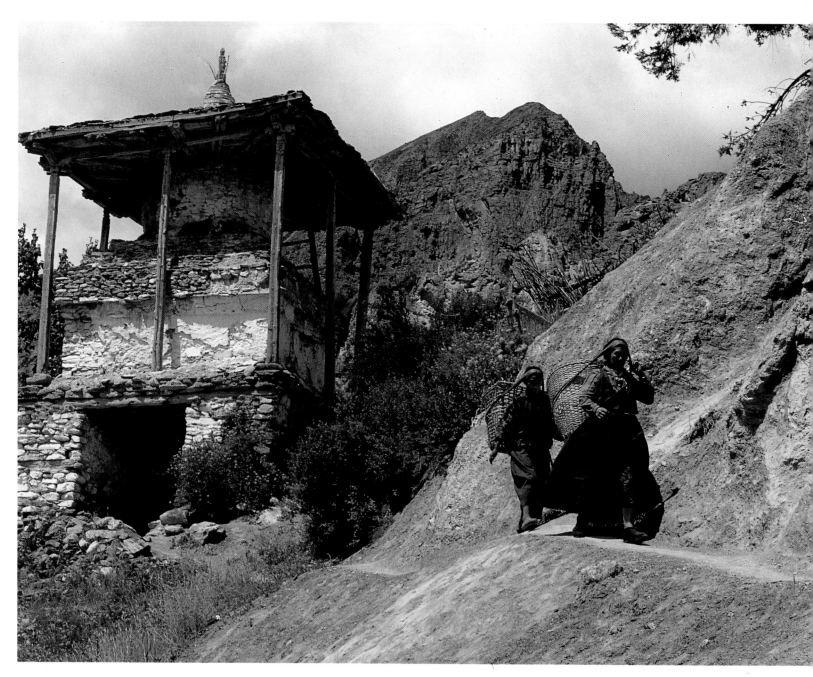

164. Long journeys on foot carrying heavily-laden baskets are the sole means of transporting goods throughout most of the Himalayas.

165. A young girl carries her 'doko' (a type of basket) on a trail between Ghyaru and Ngawal, in the Nyasyang region, the upper portion of the Manang Valley. In the background: the village of Ghyaru, clinging to an arid slope, and the towering Pisang peak (6,091 m.).

166. *The village of Ngawal (3,650 m.) in the Nyasyang region with typical flat-roofed stone dwellings, with prayer-flags fluttering in last rays of cool December sunshine (overleaf).*

167. *No fear of heights inhibits the dwellers of the Himalayan regions. A family crosses the slender suspension bridge spanning a deep gorge of the Marsyandi River in the Annapurna region of Nepal. (pp. 216-7)*

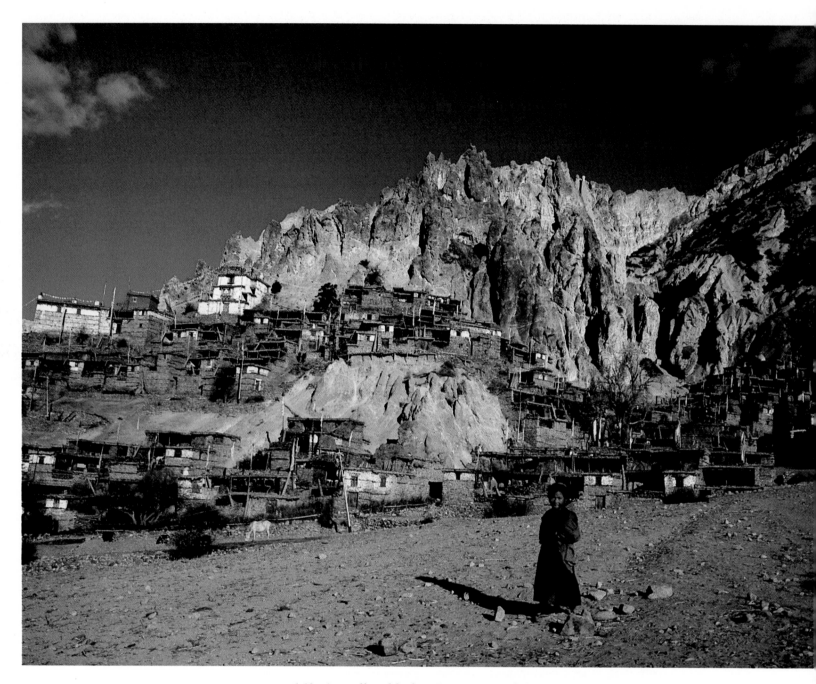

168. A small girl before Braga, one of the most picturesque villages of the Annapurna region. The gompa, perched on a crag above the village and scarcely distinguishable from the rock, is one of the largest in the district.

169. *Sunlit houses, each with its prayer flag, cluster round the village gompa, at the foot of an enormous rock face called Paungda Danda, in the upper Pisang region.*

170, 171. The village of Braga (above and right), a cluster of some 200 houses at an altitude of 3,500 m. in the Manang district of the Annapurna region. Its Manangi inhabitants are of Tibetan stock. The houses are stacked one on top of the other, with the flat roof serving as the open verandah of the house above.

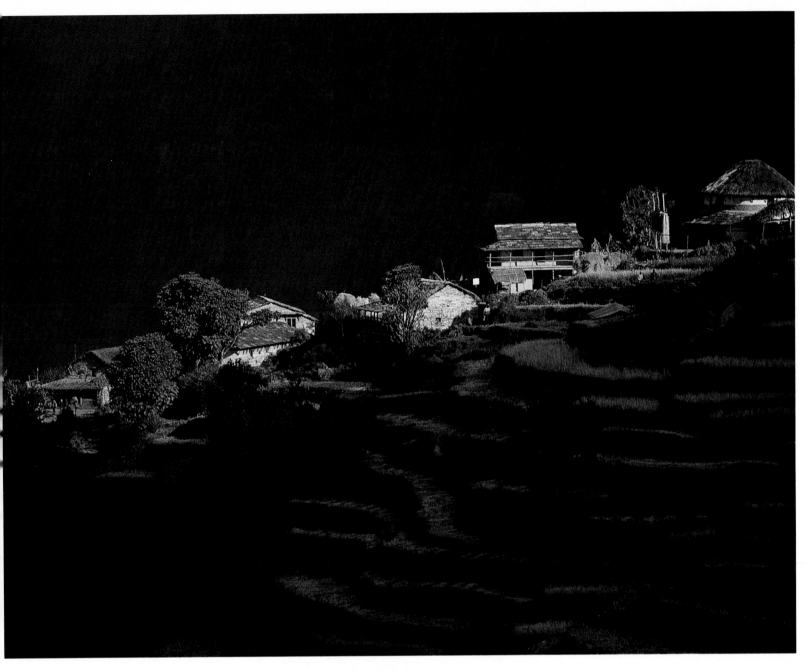

*172. A hillside hamlet of Gurung houses
near Pokhara. Some 85,000 Gurungs live
in Nepal, mostly in the eastern and
central regions. They make up the largest
component of the Gurkhas, the renowned
soldiers of the British and Indian armies,
who are also drawn from a number of
other tribes of the area.*

173-176. Men and beasts of burden provide the only possible form of land transport in these rugged regions of Nepal. Top and bottom pictures: a caravan of pack animals heading down the Thak Khola Valley.

177. The trail through the Kali Gandaki Valley is a major trade route leading to Mustang and further north to Tibet. All the way along there are caravans of donkeys and hardy ponies, the animals most suited to this steep terrain (opposite).

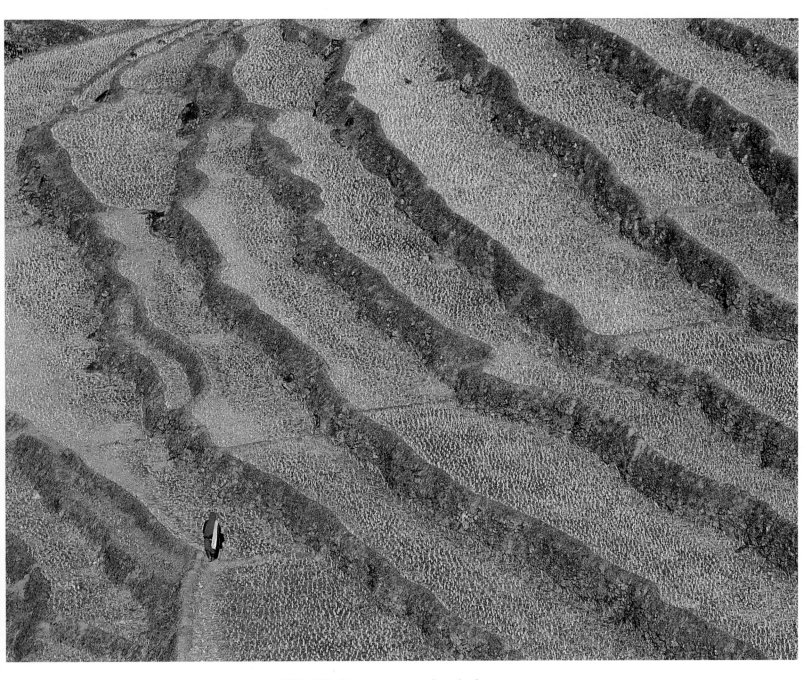

178, 179. Rice terraces after the harvest below the village of Bagarchap in the Manang Valley. The immense labour invested in the building and maintaining of these terraces, added to that of the back-breaking toil of cultivating this crop, is testimony enough to the tenacity and industry of the villagers and countless generations of their ancestors.

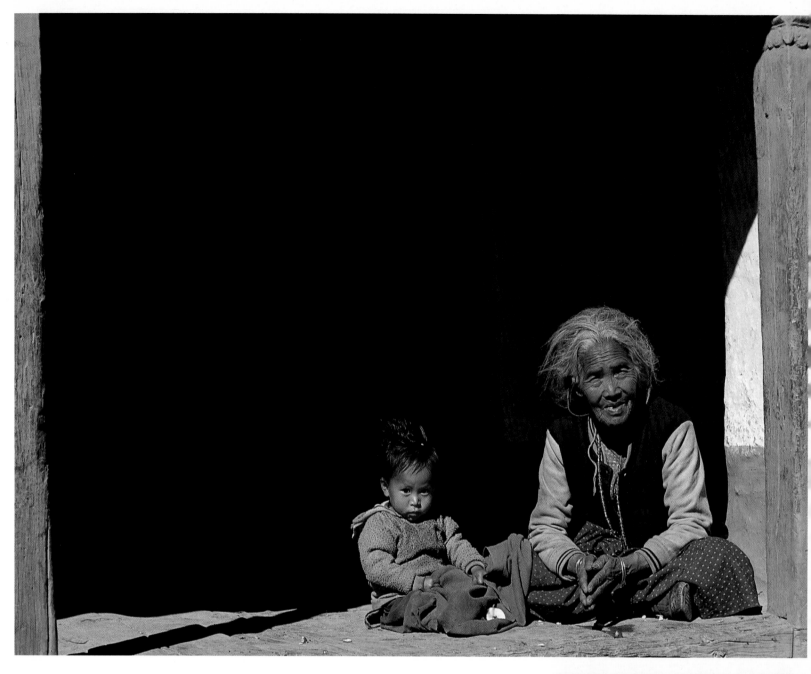

180. *A woman with her grandson in Marpha, a large village in the upper Kali Gandaki Valley inhabited by Thakali, who are noted as salt traders.*

181. *A Manangi girl from Braga enjoys a bowl of rice. The birthrate is high in Nepal, and the fertile lowland Terai region, where 40 per cent of Nepalese live, is very densely populated.*

*182. An elderly Gurung from Ngawal
absorbed in prayer. About 90 per cent of
the Nepali are Hindu, but often
Hinduism, the state religion, is closely
intertwined with Buddhism.*

183. *This brother and sister live with their mother in a small bhatti (tea-house) near Chhomro, on the way to the Annapurna Sancutary.*

184. *A Manangi woman grinding grain at a watermill near the town of Manang. Rice is grown up to an altitude of about 2,000 m., maize up to 2,900 m, and barley as high as 4,400 m.*

185. *A common scene in Nepalese everyday life: a small child looking after the new baby. Responsibility comes early in large families where the mother has many chores in addition to work on the land.*

186. A honey hunter from the foothills of the Annapurna region of Nepal. The loose cape is his only protection against the swarms of bees he disturbs.

187, 188. Gurung honey hunters crossing a swift mountain stream, one of them carrying a brood comb on his back. In the past, mountain-dwellers relied on honey as the only source of sweetness in their diet.

189. Hanging on a rope ladder, with only a thin cord around his waist to secure him, a honey hunter plunges his bamboo pole into the bees' nest, driving out the swarm. No wonder this risky and strenuous occupation is dying out.

190. A young honey hunter (above) who is learning the craft from his father.

The next year, 1922, saw another expedition, this one led by Charles Bruce, who had climbed with Mummery on Nanga Parbat in 1895. He was now fifty-six and brought matchless experience to a party comprising 14 other Britons, 50 Sherpas and 100 Tibetans. By early May, a camp was established at Rongbuk and in a series of attempts made along the East Rongbuk Glacier and the North Col, the strongest climbers reached 27,300 ft (8,531 m.), only 2,000 ft below the summit and higher than any man had previously gone. At 8 a.m. on June 7, four separately-roped parties set out to cross the steep slopes below the North Col. Suddenly the snow above avalanched, engulfing and sweeping away all 17 climbers. Seven of the Sherpas were thrown into a crevasse and killed. The expedition was abandoned after the worst accident there had been on Everest, a tragedy which tempered enthusiasm for the notable accomplishments that preceded it.

The third expedition to Everest, in 1924, got off to a bad start when the leader, Bruce again, was taken ill with malaria whilst the party was trekking towards Tibet. He was forced to return, replaced by Edward Norton (1884-1954), who was responsible for 10 Britons, 55 Sherpas and 150 Tibetans. The bad omens continued when, in early May, two Sherpas were killed by a blizzard which wrecked their camp. Norton reached 28,126 ft (8,789 m.), but was forced down by the treacherous ground ahead of him and snow-blindness, which did not leave him for three days. His achievement was to remain the world altitude record for thirty years, until the Swiss expedition of 1952, when Raymond Lambert and Tenzing Norgay went higher on another face.

Following Norton's attempt, Mallory chose Andrew Irvine, a twenty-two-year-old with only modest experience, to accompany him on a climb to the top. On the morning of June 8, they set out. A fellow member of the expedition, N. Odell, sighted them above 27,000 ft (8,400 m.), and that was the last time they were ever seen. In 1933 an ice-axe belonging to them was found, reviving the debate as to whether they could have reached the summit. Hillary and Tenzing looked briefly for signs of them when they made their successful ascent, but given the eternally changing face of the slopes, along with their priorities on that day, it is not surprising they found no trace.

Quite the most fascinating speculation on their subsequent fate is set out in Ian Cameron's book *Mountain of the Gods*, in which he points out that both Mallory and Irvine carried cameras loaded with Eastman Kodak film. The manufacturer is certain that if the film were found, recognisable prints could be developed, and since Mallory and Irvine would certainly have taken photographs from the summit had they reached it, the discovery of the bodies and cameras could solve the puzzle. Cameron records that Chinese climbers found a body on Everest in 1975 'dressed in old-fashioned and disintegrating kit'. The Chinese have never officially admitted finding a westerner, although they did report retrieving the body of a Chinese climber who fell to his death just below the summit in 1975. To the question of whether Mallory and Irvine reached the summit, we can add three more: did the Chinese find one of their bodies, was there a camera with film that could be developed, and if so, why have the Chinese remained steadfastly silent?

Whatever the truth of the matter, their deaths probably influenced the

191. A girl fetching water from the stream near the village of Bhratang, now largely abandoned, in the upper valley of the Marsyandi River. When the snows melt, this will become a raging torrent and fetching water will not be child's play.

decision of the Tibetan Government to withdraw permission to climb on the mountain for eight years. Requests were made for an attempt from the Nepalese face but, as before, they were rejected. The Dalai Lama finally yielded to diplomatic persuasion and the next expedition was launched in 1933. That year the mountain was dogged by exceptionally bad weather, without a lull in which to mount a serious assault upon the summit. By mid-June, the expedition had withdrawn. Two years later, Eric Shipton (1907-1977) led a light-weight reconnaissance team of six climbers and 15 Sherpas. One of them was Tenzing Norgay, a twenty-one-year-old joining his first major expedition and carrying loads up to heights of 22,000 ft, which was as high as the team reached. All that he saw and did confirmed that climbing was in his blood and, although an apprentice, he had the flair as well as the ambition to go higher, even to the top.

Nanda Devi. Nanda Devi (the Blessed Goddess), at 25,643 ft (7,816 m.) the highest mountain in the Commonwealth, was first climbed on August 29, 1936, by H. Tilman and N. Odell, two outstanding British climbers who were members of a joint Anglo-American team. Eric Shipton, a great friend of Tilman, was away making a reconnaissance on Everest at the time. Both wrote excellent books about their climbing experiences and were strong advocates of small, light expeditions rather than large teams supported by hundred of porters shifting tons of supplies. Another celebrity who climbed the Himalayas in the 1930s was F. Spencer Chapman, who scaled Chomolhari, 23,997 ft (7,499 m.) in 1937. Subsequently, for three and a half years he organised a guerrilla campaign against the Japanese within Malaya, where he stayed behind after the occupation; his account of his adventures, *The Jungle is Neutral*, was another best-seller.

The 1930s had seen many tragedies, balanced by considerable achievements. Only a few peaks had been climbed, but a good many had been attempted and a great deal learnt about the kind of organisation required, the approaches that offered the best chance of reaching the summit, and the value of the Sherpa as a tenacious, knowledgeable and indefatigable companion.

All serious climbing in the mountains came to an end for the duration of the Second World War, and the partition of India and Pakistan in 1947 led to the consequent prohibition of Indian nationals, such as Sherpas, from climbing in the Western Himalayas embraced by Pakistan. It was the opening of Nepal's borders to mountaineers that signalled the achievements that were to come in the 1950s and the ascent of most of the highest peaks.

Annapurna. The best period for climbing is between mid-May and mid-June, although an early monsoon can throw all such calculations haywire. In 1950 a French expedition led by Maurice Herzog made an early start on Annapurna, 26,546 ft (8,091 m.), partly in order to familiarise themselves with the conditions and partly to survey the best approach. Not until mid-May was the route up decided upon, but by the end of the month a camp was established at 23,500 ft (7,343 m.), from which the final assault could be launched. Margins for errors in timing assaults are lean, and a forecast predicting an early monsoon now injected even greater energy into the team.

Herzog and another member of the expedition, Louis Lachenal, spent the night of June 2 on a steep slope within 2,000 ft (625 m.) of the summit. Outside their tent a storm raged, but by 6 a.m. the next day the weather had cleared, giving a fine blue sky, accompanied by searing cold, for the final climb. The two Frenchmen slogged upwards and by 2 p.m. reached their goal. They had made the highest ascent in the world and were the first men to go above 8,000 m. (26,246 ft). Then things began to go wrong. Good visibility gave way to an ominous overcast heralding a storm. In the violent blizzard which began to rage, Herzog lost both his gloves and contact with his companion—to save weight they had begun the day without a rope. Herzog reached their camp, where two fellow climbers waited for them, but Lachenal went past the camp. It was his cries for help when he fell 300 ft that attracted attention and led to his rescue.

Their descent the next day was painful and dangerous; they were experiencing frost-bite and lost their way in newly fallen snow. Almost providentially, at dusk Lachenal fell into a shallow crevasse, into which the others climbed and spent a night of misery marooned in snow. In the early morning more snow from an avalanche almost buried them, but with brightening weather Herzog and Lachenal, both badly frost-bitten, and their two companions, who were totally snow-blind, reached a lower camp where a doctor could treat them. Lachenal lost his toes; Herzog his fingers and toes. Despite this handicap, Herzog excited the admiration of Tenzing Norgay for the way he drove his car in Chamonix, when the two met some years afterwards.

Everest, the Conquest. Among the main contenders in the battle to claim the peaks, the sublime heights of Everest always represented the major prize. In November 1950, Tilman and Charles Houston, an American professor of medicine who specialised in high-altitude physiology, made a first reconnaissance, entering Nepal accompanied by four Sherpas. From the foot of the Khumbu Glacier, Tilman echoed Mallory's pessimistic observation about a southern approach expressed thirty years earlier. The next year, Shipton led five climbers and 15 Sherpas for another look. This time the expedition set out in September, and on the 30th, Shipton and Edmund Hillary were at 20,000 ft (6,250 m.) on a ridge of Pumori, 23,190 ft (7,247 m.), when they looked towards Everest some five or six miles away. In Hillary's words: 'To my astonishment the whole valley lay revealed to our eyes. A long, narrow, snowy trough swept from the top of the ice-fall and climbed steeply up the face of Lhotse... And even as the same thought was simmering in my own mind, Shipton said, "There's a route there!"'

Shipton made a report on his successful discovery when he returned to London and preparations were begun for the next expedition in 1953. The Swiss Foundation for Alpine Research had obtained permission to climb on Everest in the spring and autumn of 1952, so that the British plan to climb that year had to be postponed. It is not hard to imagine the mixed emotions of the British when the first Swiss attempt failed. They climbed for the second time in November. In sub-zero temperatures and a rising winter gale, Raymond Lambert and Tenzing Norgay reached within 500 ft (160 m.) of the peak and then had to descend. The party had been strong, well-organised and well-equipped; Lambert and Tenzing were two of the finest climbers alive, with a strong bond of mutual trust and liking for each other, but they were climbing too late: Everest drove them down. The race to the top was still on, and to underline the consequences of a British failure in 1953, the Swiss and the French were booked to climb in 1954 and 1955.

Led by Colonel John Hunt, the expedition, planned with military thoroughness, consisted of 10 climbers and 33 Sherpa porters. The *sirdar* (leader) of the latter was Tenzing Norgay. Now thirty-nine, he had begun on Everest in 1935, and had climbed in the Hindu Kush as well as on mountains such as Nanga Parbat, Nanda Devi and Kabru. He was made a full member of the climbing team for this, his seventh attempt on that isolated peak with its familiar spindrift trailing away into the thin air. On May 27, Charles Evans, a surgeon and deputy leader of the expedition, accompanied by Tom Bourdillon, a physicist who had helped develop the

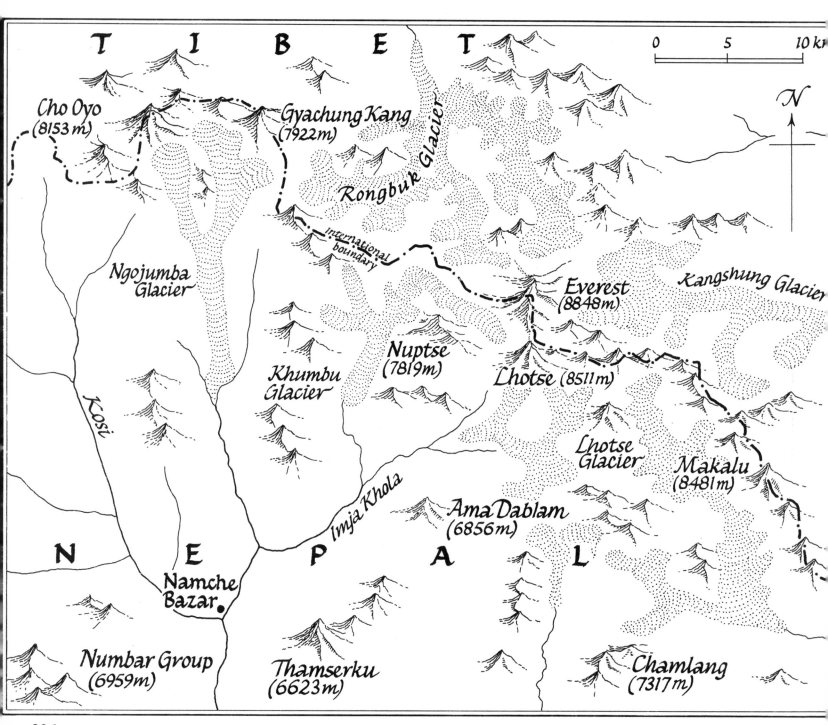

oxygen apparatus being used, climbed within 300 ft (100 m.) of the summit, but were compelled by exhaustion to return to camp.

They had pioneered the way forward and it now fell to Edmund Hillary and Tenzing Norgay to put in their assault. At 2.30 p.m. the next day they watched as two other climbers and a Sherpa deposited their loads, wished them luck, and started down back to camp. Hillary and Tenzing began clearing the snow in the lee of an exposed rock as a prelude to erecting a tent on the highest place a camp had ever been pitched. Because of altitude fatigue, everything took five times longer than normal, but the wind was light and conditions inside the tent enabled them to remove their gloves without fear of frost-bite. Tenzing fired up the stove and made warm coffee and lemon juice, while Hillary checked their oxygen sets and cylinders. They dozed fitfully. At 3.30 a.m. they began to prepare for the final assault. They boiled snow to mix with lemon-juice and coffee, ate a little of the previous night's left-overs, and rejoiced to find the wind had died out to leave a fine morning with visibility equal to the fabulous views in all directions. By 6.30 a.m., burdened only by the 40 pounds of oxygen apparatus they each carried, they quit the tent and started upwards.

Two bottles of oxygen left by Evans and Bourdillon were gratefully found and the site noted. They then encountered soft snow which slowed their progress. Just as they found harder snow, they had the additional good fortune of each finishing an oxygen bottle and immediately travelled 20 pounds lighter when they uncoupled them and left them behind. By 11.30 they had reached the top. In Hillary's famous words: ' I waved Tenzing up to me. A few more whacks of the ice-axe, and we were on the summit of Everest.' Tenzing held up the flags of the United Nations, Britain, Nepal and India on his ice-axe and Hillary took the famous photograph. Under the deepest of blue skies and above a horizon extending for hundreds of miles they saw the way the gentle breeze from Tibet wooed the flimsy plumes of spindrift, Everest's trademark, westerly above the Khumbu Glacier and the hills and valleys of Tenzing's birthplace. The two men drew on their sibilant respirators and looked at the great Himalayas as no others had done, gazing down on stupendous giants such as Lhotse, Makalu, Nuptse and Kanchenjunga.

After fifteen minutes they started back down the mountain, taking their first steps toward immortality, an immortality which happened to reverberate with the coronation bells of Queen Elizabeth II and augur well for her reign. The climbers had thought their triumph would be totally overshadowed by events in London. In fact, the pomp and circumstance of the one was enhanced by the courage and achievement of the other. The descent went according to the careful planning and by June 20 everyone was safely down and comfortably quartered in Kathmandu. The expedition had benefited from earlier experience, used excellent equipment, kept in good health, maintained a close-knit sense of unity and, above all, the weather had been particularly fine for the last two weeks of May. Nine climbers had gone to the South Col, seven of whom went on to 27,000 ft (8,440 m.), four climbed to 28,700 ft (8,970 m.) and two to the top. Some 750 pounds of stores were lifted to 26,000 ft (8,125 m.) by the Sherpas who were, in Lord Hunt's words, 'magnificent'.

Neither the climbers, nor Everest, nor the Himalayas would ever be the same. In 1991, an attempt to ski down the mountain led to fatalities and was abandoned. It is now proposed to take the first tourists, with previous climbing experience, up to 23,000 ft (7,187 m.), on a guided tour that will follow the South Col route taken by Hillary and Tenzing.

The mountain has since been climbed by Swiss, Americans, Indians, Italians, Japanese—among them Juko Tabei, the first woman to reach the summit, a Tibetan woman, Phantog, Chinese, the British on a new and particularly difficult face, Nepalese, South Koreans, Austrians, Germans, French and by Reinhold Messner solo, without oxygen equipment. This same feat was achieved in 1995 by the British woman climber Allison Hargreaves, who lost her life after reaching the summit of K2 a few weeks later.

Solo Ascents. The latter half of the Fifties saw the conquest of seven other major peaks: Lhotse, Makalu, Manaslu, Cho Oyo, Gasherbrum I and II and Broad Peak, and when two more followed in the Sixties, the scene was set for the revolutionary Reinhold Messner. Born in the Italian-occupied Tyrol in 1944, Messner soon acquired a reputation for outstanding solo ascents on exacting Alpine faces, using almost no aids such as pegs or small portable steps. His first Himalayan climb was on Nanga Parbat in 1970. He and his brother Gunther reached the summit, but Gunther was unwell and they descended by the little-known Diamiri Face, looking down on the Diamiri Glacier—one of the most difficult climbs in the world. Climbing, as was Messner's custom, without ropes, camps or oxygen, they were almost down when Gunther was killed by an avalanche.

In 1975 Reinhold began a partnership with the Austrian Peter Habeler. Using their Alpine 'free-climbing' style, they successfully ascended Gasherbrum I. Three years later the two men climbed Everest without oxygen and, as if to drive the point home, in 1980 Messner climbed Everest from the Chinese side, without oxygen and solo. When he climbed Gasherbrum solo in 1984, he came close to tragedy, yet survived a bad fall and rock avalanche. In a ten-day period in August 1982 he climbed alone to the summits of Broad Peak and Gasherbrum II.

In 1986 he reached his fourteenth peak above 8,000 m., Lhotse, and by doing so completed a task he had set himself when he began climbing. His achievements overturned much earlier thinking and set new waymarks for climbing solo or in small groups. He dispensed with carefully thought-out, military-style preparations and used virtually no equipment, regarding oxygen as of little help. Emphatically he led by example. The fact that by 1990 only one other mountaineer had emulated his blitzkrieging feats puts his audacious achievements in some perspective.

The sobering figures show that 2.1 per cent of all climbers on Everest between spring 1971 and December 1985 perished, and that Annapurna I by December 1985 had claimed 43 lives for the 36 persons who had reached its peak. It is a high price for fifteen minutes with a camera, preoccupied by the problems of a zig-zag descent through ice-encrusted snow, threatened by frost-bite, partially blinded by the reflected glare, and aware of the capriciousness of the environment. As amazing as the mountains themselves is the human characteristic of climbing them for the sake of it, forever encapsulated in Hillary's memorable reply when asked why he wanted to climb Mount Everest: 'Because it's there.'

LIVING ON THE HEIGHTS

*' The lives of those who inherit our mountain-
ous areas are far from romantic. The people are simple and sincere but every problem acquires complexity
because of the altitude, the shortage of water and lack
of communication. As one who loves the mountains, I
have a deep concern for the mountain people. In order
to survive, they must have great faith and fortitude.
They are strong and hardworking, yet full of laughter
and gaiety.'*

Indira Gandhi (1917-1984)

Communications. The rigours of the region were described as early
as 1334 in the writings of one of the greatest medieval travellers, Ibn
Batuta, who gave the first recorded explanation of the name Hindu Kush:
'Another motive for our stoppage was the fear of snow, for there is mid-
way on the road a mountain called Hindu Kush, i.e. the Hindu Killer,
because so many slaves, male and female, brought from India, die in the
passage of this mountain, owing to the severe cold and quantity of snow.'

Unforgettable as the heights may be, with their frozen glaciers, isolated valleys and rare flora and fauna, no less remarkable are the forty million people of the high Himalayas, living in small tribal communities,
their fragile cohesion maintained by the sensitive mechanisms of trade
and the stability of their faiths. Among the mountains, most foreigners
feel they are voyeurs in a strange private world. Yet there regularly shines
through a unique harmony with nature that, despite the isolation of the
diverse peoples and their cultures, provides the strength and simplicity
needed to live on the Roof of the World.

It is, however, generally surprising to discover how accessible the
mountains have been over the centuries to unnumbered pilgrims, traders,
soldiers, missionaries, or simply the inhabitants moving animals for better
pasture. An intricate system of valleys provides adequate means of communication. Best known is the Khyber Pass, but growing importance
attaches to the recent linking of passes along the Karakorum Highway,
412 miles (6,56 km.) in length, which runs all the way to China via the
Khunjerab Pass at 16,300 ft (4,934 m.). The Karakorum Highway follows
the Indus River valley; some forty miles to the east is the Kunhar River
and the Babusar Pass, 14,850 ft (4,500 m.). Before the partition of India,
this area lay on the traditional route to Srinagar in Kashmir. Srinagar
(City of Shri, the happy woman, otherwise known as Lakshmi, wife of
Vishnu), is linked in turn with Leh, capital of Ladakh, by the Zoji La
Pass at 12,200 ft (3,700 m.). North from Leh, bordering the contested
Aksai Chin area, is the Karakorum Pass, 18,400 ft, (5,575 m.). All these
passes lay along routes and feeder arteries of the ancient Silk Road, fol-
lowed by Marco Polo, by which the rich caravans of China and Central
Asia supplied the bazaars of the sub-continent.

Over lunch in Delhi with that great traveller and expert on Himalayan

192. A view from the pastures of Lhabarma (4,328 m.), on the way from Namche Bazar to Gokyo peak (5,483 m.), towards Kangtega (6,779 m.). The name, meaning 'snow saddle', seems more appropriate when the mountain is viewed from Thangboche.

193. Two sunlit beauties of the Solo-Khumbu region, Kangtega (6,779 m.) and Thamserku (6,623 m.), glimpsed between swirling dark clouds (overleaf). Such dramatic contrasts and sudden changes of weather are frequent at these altitudes.

194. Namche Bazar, a village that has become famous through climbing expeditions, is a trading centre for Solo-Khumbu region below Everest, the homeland of the Sherpas. The horseshoe-shaped village is dominated by the magnificent Kwangde range (6,011 m.). (pp. 244-5)

anthropology, Professor Christophe von Furer-Haimendorf, I heard a striking illustration of how sensitive the passes further east can be. Asked about the situation along the Nepal-Tibet border, he recalled the impact on trade when Tibet closed its border in 1959. Trans-Himalayan traders from Nepal had regularly negotiated the frontier, leading pack-sheep and goats through the high passes to buy salt; sealing the borders caused the merchants to look southwards, towards India, where rice could be bartered for salt and the route was not as difficult. Their resourcefulness shortly led to the border being opened for limited commerce, despite the political tensions that had created the situation in the first place. It is sad to reflect that the once fabulously rich Cathay of the Silk Road should have bothered to interfere with a trifling amount of trade across menacing passes where men and animals trek for weeks on end.

Environmental Threats. Almost all who visit the Himalayas are surprised that the omnipresent poverty niggles their conscience as little as it does. It is the politeness, dignity and friendship of the people that remain in the mind, along with a willingness to share a unique environment, their culture and religions. The enterprise of Sir Edmund Hillary, involved for over thirty years in projects involving twenty-five schools, two hospitals, ten medical clinics, bridges, fresh water and reforestation, is a celebrated example of a visitor who, whilst recognising the uncomplaining attitude of the people, determined to improve their circumstances. International aid-donors have allocated funds for schools, hospitals and roads, but there is an understandable reluctance to tamper too much with what is a self-reliant and essentially civil kind of paradise. Difficulties are shouldered in the Himalayas with little sense of grievance; faith may not move mountains, but it does the next best thing, it makes them inhabitable, and one must admit that fatalism, that close relative of backwardness, is an invaluable trait where gods are unfathomable and capricious.

Environmental problems threaten the Himalayas just as they menace other parts of the planet. Here the root cause of these is population growth, though average life expectancy is no more than fifty-two years. More people means an increased demand for basic necessities: fuel and food. It has been estimated, for example, that 90 per cent of the wood taken from the forests of Nepal is for fuel, and unless vast reforestation schemes are carried out, the country could be denuded of trees by the end of the century. The threat is, of course, most keenly felt in those places where it is most desirable to live. Charcoal (which has better heat-generating qualities than wood) is cheaper than coal from the plains. Annual demand in the Darjeeling Hills is for three million bags weighing 10 kilos each, while local production runs to 120,000 bags.

When Darjeeling was taken over by the East India Company from the Rajah of Sikkim in 1835, there were only 100,000 inhabitants living there. By 1981, attracted by the economic growth related to extensive tea plantations, over a million people lived in the area, 38 per cent of whom lived off lumbering and 22.5 per cent from the tea industry. Though Darjeeling means place or town of thunderbolts, the desirability of living there is testified by the fact it was once the summer headquarters of the Bengal Government and sanatorium of eastern India. Mount Everest is visible from Darjeeling, so too is Kanchenjunga, with a summit of exposed granite too sheer for snow to settle; other Himalayan giants

195. *The warm light of the setting sun makes the cutting edges of Cholatse (6,440 m.) and Tawetse (6,542 m.) even sharper.*

196. *The mighty massif of Kangtega (opposite), seen from pastureland near Laza, on the way to Gokyo peak.*

197. The yak is indispensable in the harsh, precipitous world of Solo-Khumbu (overleaf). Besides carrying supplies along the narrow trails high above the turbulent rivers, it ploughs fields and provides milk for butter, wool for clothing, leather for shoes, and dung for fuel.

198. Each Saturday there is an important 'hat' or market in Namche Bazar, where corn, rice, eggs, vegetables, and produce not grown in Khumbu are on sale. The focus of the region's trade, it brings together a colourful throng. Sherpas from all the neighbouring villages come to meet friends and relatives. (pp. 250-1)

199. The hardy soles of a porter's feet never wear out.

200. Produce is carried to Namche Bazar from villages six to ten days' walk away by lowland porters.

201. As sturdy as the men, Sherpanis carry heavy loads up and down hills. Broad head-bands help support the weight.

202. Porters belong to the lowest social stratum in Nepal. They spend their lives toting heavy burdens, and many waste their earnings on gambling or drink.

203. A Rai maiden, adorned in traditional jewelry, from the large village of Jubing on the way from Jiri to Namche Bazar. The Rai are an ancient Nepalese ethnic group who speak a Tibetan-Burmese language.

204, 205. *Tibetans (above and left) are always present at the Saturday market in Namche Bazar, buying, selling and exchanging goods.*

206. *An old Thakali (far left) from the Kali Gandaki region with a typical cape over his head.*

254

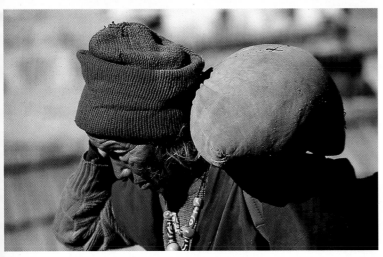

207. *A small chorten on the way between Ghyaru and Ngawal in the Annapurna region, with a prayer-wheel turned by water, when the stream is not frozen.*

208. *Porters journeying from Jiri to Namche Bazar, Solo-Khumbu, Nepal.*

209. *After buying supplies at the market, an old Sherpa leaving for his village at the foot of the highest Himalayan peaks.*

tower along a fabulous horizon. Apart from the tea-gardens, oak, chestnuts and magnolia, tree-ferns, palms and rhododendrons flourish; rice, maize and millet are grown, as well as a range of superb vegetables which bring cosmopolitan groups of Tibetans, Nepalese, Bhotias, Bengalis and Marwaris in increasing numbers to trade and enjoy a city well supplied with hydro-electric power. The exploitation of water power at least reduces the need to burn and destroy forests in order to cook and keep warm.

As more people live at altitude, another serious problem arises. Deforestation, whether to obtain fuel or arable land, leads to soil erosion: Nepal 'exports' 240 million cubic metres of soil every year. The sight of the Himalayan rivers carrying in suspension vast quantities of soil tells its own worrying story. While some usefully settles in the Ganges plain, the rest can be seen 400 miles out to sea discolouring the Bay of Bengal. And once soil erosion reaches naked rock, reforestation is impossible. It was once thought that the 'slash and burn' cycle in the eastern Himalayas lasted about twenty-five years; in some areas this has shrunk to four or five years and poses a grave threat. The Western Himalayas' impoverished slopes present a visible example of the result of shifting cultivation. In Nepal the annual population increase is 1.8 per cent per year, in areas where only 10 per cent of the land is arable. It is estimated that it takes from five hundred to a thousand years to form an inch of top-soil; in a matter of minutes, carefully ploughed and nurtured terraced slopes on steep hillsides can be flushed away by a monsoon downpour. In addition, the removal of ground cover by those practising shifting cultivation in Sikkim, Bhutan and Arunachal Pradesh, or those cutting trees to float downstream to sawmills, leaves the soil directly exposed to weathering. Moreover, overstocking cattle—and what could be more natural than a hill-man's desire to increase his flock of sheep, goats or yaks?—-takes an ecologically disastrous toll of the rough grazing available.

Another factor is the erosion of the glaciers which, in the case of the Baltoro Glacier south-east of K2 in the Karakorums, can be as much as six feet in a day, whilst the Khumbu, south-west of Mount Everest, recedes by about a foot daily. Glaciers are, of course, always in movement, only rarely becoming stationary when cycles of melting and freezing cancel each other out. Global warming may be the cause in the present age.

A visitor should not be deceived by the smiles, the hardihood, fatalism and faith, or the number of bangles and necklaces worn by the women. Life in the mountains is full of hardship, an endless struggle for survival, but in a curious way the stumbling-blocks in the way of solutions among this patchwork of tribes, regions and nations may have prevented a man-made disaster. A thousand miles north-west of the Karakorums lies what was once the fourth largest body of inland water, the Aral Sea. Since 1960 the level of the lake has fallen 50 ft (15 m.) and its main port is now 60 miles (100 km.) from the water. Centrally planned irrigation and hydro-electric schemes have set in train a catastrophe affecting almost as many people (33 million) as those who live in the high Himalayas. The latter may have a great deal to contend with, but fortunately, a centralised bureaucracy with executive authority but no intention of living in the region, is not one of them.

210. A ten-year-old boy and his baby brother in the doorway of their home in Mali, a small Sherpa settlement at 2,200 m. The garlands are an offering to the gods and should bring good luck to the family.

Tradition and Change. Whilst there is an abundance of resources in the Himalayas, their consumption is a matter of widespread concern that has led to an outcry for greater conservation. Which provokes the question: why should people with so little be asked to make do with less? While age-old methods may be wasteful, how can reform be affected? No one argues against the need for environmental management and protection—clearly it is in the long-term interest of all who live there—but the progressive deepening of official involvement and the proliferation of committees, reports, investigations and research encompassing every science known to man, all focus on bringing about change on the mountainside. 'Slash and burn' made Europe inhabitable and worked for the Aryans who laid waste the forests bordering the Ganges on their march eastwards. Not surprisingly, the people of the mountains trust the tribal or village economy which regulates their arduous way of life. The fact they themselves have not found improvement easy makes them understandably dubious about the guidance of outsiders.

An abiding lesson is the example of Tibet. For the British who ruled India, Tibet made an ideal buffer state between India and tsarist Russia. Later Tibet came to be regarded as a buffer between India and China. Nehru inherited this situation in 1947 when India gained independence. Ironically, as a man who had dedicated his life to anti-imperialism, he wanted no part in guaranteeing Tibetan autonomy. Following the Chinese invasion of Tibet, one of the first acts of the new rulers was to station troops along the borders with India, Burma, Pakistan and Russia and close all frontiers. In late 1957 it was discovered that the Chinese had built a road between Sinkiang and Tibet which crossed vast stretches of Indian territory in Aksai Chin. When the Chinese stepped up their programme of modernisation in Tibet, the Dalai Lama took refuge in India and the situation came to a head in 1962 with a border conflict in the Himalayas between the two largest Asian nations.

Once the military clash was over, China set about the reforms in Tibet in earnest. Like the majority of peoples in the Himalayas, the Tibetans are extraordinarily alert to their environment; they revere nature and seek to establish a harmonious balance between their way of life and the spiritual forces with which they share their country. They are no more free of shortcomings than any other people, but they are generally affable and confident of their intimate contact with mountains, soil, animals and crops. The monasteries and their inmates, worship and ceremony, play a central social, religious and economic role.

All of this was anathema to the Chinese, who began disbanding the monasteries and putting their inmates, who were considered parasites, into productive employment. Buddhist scripture, myths and legends were to be replaced by Marxism. On the credit side, they poured in money to build schools, hospitals and roads, but also state farms, factories and other debatable benefits of twentieth-century civilisation. Industrialisation, it was thought, would help create a new class, the new proletariat. The plan failed. Perhaps changes will come, but for the majority of the population, the switch to Marxist atheism and the concept of transition from the seventh to the twentieth century in a few decades were too much to swallow. Popular resistance led to the adoption of a more liberal attitude in the 1980s, and the state has become more tolerant of organised religion. Whether Chinese expectations were too high or Tibetan conservatism too ingrained is a moot point. Certainly the Chinese underestimated the Tibetans' tenacious devotion to their way of life and their reluctance to change. There is more than one path to enlightenment.

Although China's approach to the problems of the region may have been misguided and less than successful, there is general agreement that the Himalayas' ancient cultures, forests and wildlife are under threat. So much may be easily acknowledged, but among the experts who identify the danger there is nothing like the same unanimity regarding the scale of the problems and how to tackle them. For a start there is the vexed issue of whether the best solution—despite the Chinese experience—is a strong, centralised, bureaucratic direction, or a decentralised system with local interests fully represented and the pace of change maintained at a locally acceptable tempo. Between these extremes there are many ways forward.

Maitreya, the Buddha who is to come, who lives in the Tusita heaven until his time to be born on earth.

Agriculture and Forestry. Despite the generally inhospitable terrain and severe climate characteristic of the Himalayan region, there are areas with rich arable land. Kashmir and the Kulu Valley grow superb apples, plums, peaches, pears and cherries which are readily sold in India. Rice, corn (maize), millet and wheat are grown on the alluvial riversides and foothills. Nepal grows one per cent of the world's output of rice and Sikkim supplies all West Bengal and Bihar's needs for seed potatoes. Known as Sikkim's Fairy Godmother and Salvation is the cardamom, a strong, spicy, aromatic seed used in curries, which is cultivated in plantations but also found growing wild on shaded mountainsides. Skirting the foot of the mountains around Darjeeling are the tea plantations, the biggest cash crop in the Himalayas. In southern Bhutan, the home of many Nepalese immigrants, bananas and oranges are grown for the Indian market. In Sikkim, 95 per cent of the population depend upon agriculture and self-sufficient horticulture for a livelihood.

Two-thirds of Bhutan and Sikkim, areas famed for their rhododendrons, orchids and moss-festooned forests, are still heavily wooded; timber is everywhere floated down streams to sawmills, for the manufacture of matches, paper-pulp and related products. To the west of Kashmir, in the Hindu Kush, the economy is barely above subsistence level, with only a little dried fruit, timber, mats and ropes being exported, whilst the Tibetans of the inaccessible Karakorums are nomadic herdsmen who grow a few cereals but concentrate upon the breeding of yaks, sheep and goats.

Apart from rice on the terraces, the main cereal crops are millet, which is harvested in the September-October period after the monsoon, and barley, usually harvested in April. Threshing is often a tedious process, when children drive cattle over the heads of grain strewn upon dung-hardened ground. I have seen it take about a working day to extract the grain from 80 kilos of cereal, which was subsequently winnowed in the traditional fashion by young women and girls, tossing the kernels into a light breeze from plaited straw trays. All around, rust, gold and olive-coloured slopes were silently dappled by the fleeting shadows of occasional clouds crossing a powder-blue sky; the beauty of distant, irregular, snow-canopied peaks only emphasised the toilsome, earth-bound existence down below.

Existence in the high Himalayas is a hard grind. For the most part villages are self-sufficient in staples such as maize, barley or millet, and grow some cash-crops, for example onions, garlic, ginger or coriander. A mainstay of the Tibetan and Sherpa diet is salted tea mixed with yak butter, and *tsampa*, a coarse barley flour, sometimes eaten raw but usually roasted and mixed with milk, yoghurt, tea or water to make a paste. It has the great virtue that it can be easily carried and eaten without need of a fire. For those who still live a nomadic life, driving their herds of yak and other cattle to different pastures according to the seasons, there is the opportunity to barter with the settled farmers. In prosperous times, the latter may do well enough to be consuming the harvest before last, and though a surplus may depress prices, there is so little selling or barter that the effect on a village is negligible. In regions where people cling to their traditional culture and way of life, it is the Buddhist institutions which benefit from this relative plenty. Temples and monasteries are kept in good repair and the season of feasts and festivals will be marked by drinking, dancing and merry-making, as well as by religious observances, when monks bestow blessings and say prayers.

Power and Mining. One solution to deforestation and the labour-intensive way of life would be to harness the hydro-electric potential of the Himalayan rivers, with the added advantage of providing irrigation systems. Eighty per cent of the irrigation canals in place in 1947, at the time of partition, went to Pakistan. Since then India has undertaken four major projects on Himalayan rivers, some of them supplying electricity also to Nepal and Bhutan. However, the costs are high and the useful life of dams has proved to be shorter than expected because of the silt which builds up and threatens to clog the system. Moreover, many rivers flow through more than one country and hydro-electric schemes have to take account of all existing usage so as to ensure that some inhabitants or riverside dwellers in the plains are not deprived whilst others benefit. The Brahmaputra, for example, flows through both Tibet and India and along one relatively short stretch falls from over 10,000 to less than 1,500 ft, representing the world's largest single potential source of hydro-power in an area with extremely modest needs. With its three major river systems of the Indus, the Ganges and the Brahmaputra, the Himalayas have greater power potential than can be satisfactorily used.

Mineral deposits have been located in many parts of the Himalayas, although the difficulties of the terrain, the poor roads, absence of railways and problems of maintaining transport facilities have generally made them uneconomical to extract. Low-grade coal and peat are found in Kashmir, but mining is confined to meeting local needs. Limestone is present virtually all over the mountains and when located near major towns, for example Mussoorie, is quarried for cement. Since most houses away from towns are built of timber, stone and earth, little use is made of these deposits. Alluvial gold is found in the Indus, and iron, copper and lead ores in Nepal, Bhutan and Sikkim, but exploitation is restricted by the harsh environment, the height of the mountains, the sparseness of the population, and the very real difficulties of access. Rare or precious metals and minerals may be found from time to time, but with slim chance that mining will be feasible or lead to improvement in the way of life of the local people.

Adaptation and Continuity. Dominant among the northern peoples of Nepal are the Thakalis, who live in clean, well-kept villages on the upper Kali Gandaki River,. They speak their own Tibetan-Burmese language and have absorbed versions of Hinduism and Lamaism. The Thakalis have developed as traders, at the same time operating a mixed economy of agriculture and animal husbandry. Salt and wool imported from Tibet are bartered for grain grown in middle Nepal. When the closure of the borders with Tibet sealed off much of the frontier trade through high passes, Thakali skills were diverted to increased trading in Nepal, where they have adapted to new needs. Whilst retaining a base in share-cropping, they have found new spheres for their entrepreneurial abilities by moving further south and taking part in the construction industry, politics and business. They have proved flexible in devising a system of financing based on mutual trust and in diversifying into the growing of apples, peaches, apricots, walnuts and almonds. Newly-introduced vegetables include cabbage, cauliflower, carrot, beans, tomato and onion. Men who drove mules over laborious trails have worked on road construction and gone on to buy and drive lorries.

Other ethnic groups have adapted to change in different ways and with varying success. Neighbouring Gurungs and Magars continue to enlist in the Indian and British Gurkha regiments, as they have done for more than a century, preferring the assured status conferred by a military career away from the Himalayas to the fluctuating prosperity of trade within them.

Tourism and political instability both bring, in their very different ways, new economic opportunities with the construction of roads, buildings, airfields and additional mouths to feed. Yet one affects the other and Kashmir, which overflows with nature's blessings—majestic mountains, lakes, glacier-fed rivers, Persian-style gardens, fertile soil—is unable to benefit economically as it should because of factional uncertainty. Following in the footsteps of the pilgrims, the conquerors, the mappers, the mountaineers and the hippies, a growing number of tourists have in recent decades set their sights on the Himalayas in their search for new and unusual vacation spots. Their influx has called for some modernisation of infrastructure and exerted a certain influence for change, besides bringing in valuable earnings.

Crafts. The skills of Kashmiri craftsmen are indisputable. Objects fashioned in wood, brass, silver or papier-maché, woven carpets or shawls in silk or wool, may sometimes have an over-worked or over-colourful appearance, but the brilliance of execution is unmistakable. Famous all over the world are the shawls of Kashmir (Cashmere), where embroidery and weaving have been elevated to a fine art. All illustration of this is the double-sided shawl, on which a 'right' and 'wrong' side can barely be distinguished. The shahtoosh ('king of woollens') is a shawl made from the under-fur (pashm) of pashmina goats, which live at an altitude of 14,000 ft (4,300 m.). Spun by experts, the finished product, elegantly needleworked, is as light as thistle-down, yet remarkably warm.

Tibetan craftsmen reflect in their work the national ideal of living in harmony with nature. For all that rug-making by refugees in India has attracted international interest, in the homeland the craftsmen express themselves predominantly through dress and jewellery. Both men and women wear the *chuba*, a heavy, hand-woven or sheepskin cloak, often thrown over one shoulder and belted at the waist. Draped with folds, the garment can carry personal effects, such as knives in the case of men.

Markets abound with stalls selling trinkets, amulets, pendants, necklaces, tinder-purses, daggers and finger-rings. Rosaries with 108 beads (so as to recite the name of Buddha 100 times and allow for losing count) are made of wood, seeds, bone or turquoise, and can be intricately carved. When in use, they are held in the right hand; otherwise they are wound around the left wrist or worn round the neck.

The punishing constraints of the high-altitude environment, the small villages, scattered population, mosaic of independent cultures and rigid control of frontiers will always retard any sudden reform of the economy. Moreover, there are precedents of peoples who, having learnt to rise above self-sufficiency, chose to live elsewhere: the Sherpas, for example, who have adapted to life around Darjeeling, and the Thakalis, who have moved to middle Nepal. But never, ever to be left out of any western economic equations is the profound spiritual grace the mountains have for devout men and women. As Nehru pointed out and the Chinese discovered, the Himalayas are something more than high mountains.

Buddha Shakyamuni ('Sage of the Skaya Clan'), epithet of Siddharta Gautama, depicted with his typical earth-touching gesture.

262

ARTISTIC INSPIRATION

'In the northern quarter is divine Himalaya,
the lord of mountains,
reaching from Eastern to Western Ocean,
firm as a rod to measure the earth...
There, demigods rest in the shade of the clouds
which spread like a girdle below the peaks,
but when the rains disturb them,
they fly to the sunlit summits'
Birth of the War-god
Kalidasa (fifth-century Sanskrit poet)

More than most regions, the Himalayas feed upon a cultural and intellectual past rooted in sacred legends and myths going back to unrecorded time. Structured like a vast cathedral, the mountains have an elemental echo of the organ ranging from tinkling streams to shrieking blizzards; the incense of juniper pine resin and smudge-fires; choir stalls of valleys; sanctuaries and sculpture of ice and rock. Small villages hang respectfully on hillsides looking upwards at peaks which are at once holy, menacing and otherworldly. The tangible signs of divine inspiration are the monasteries, temples, stupas, bronzes, prayer flags, prayer wheels, the garments of the religious, and the paths and places of pilgrimage, all of which enable the inhabitants both to express themselves and to celebrate their relationship with the Eternal. It therefore comes as no surprise that religious patronage has played a crucial role in the creation of art in the Himalayas, just as it has in many other parts of the world, and that religion has been the main inspiration of works of art and architecture.

Early Buddhist artists represented the Buddha only by symbols of his earthly life, such as his footprints. In north-west India from the first to the third centuries, the propagation and popularisation of Buddhism saw the Enlightened One depicted in a recognisably human form. This happened where Hellenism on its eastward path encountered Buddhism moving westwards. Gandhara was where they met, combining Greek, Roman and Persian technique with the devout stimulus of the personality of the Buddha. His images are distinguished by their serenity and semblance of bland compassion, the Hellenistic influence being marked in the treatment of the garments, their folds and the pose of the standing figure, whilst the symbolic positions of the hand and fingers, the motif of the lotus and other characteristics are unmistakably Indian in origin. Based upon the *Mahayana* texts which were composed in the region, the sculptures depict the life of the Buddha and were lodged in the stupas, around which worshippers circumambulated. In the fifth century A.D., the Huns ravaged the Peshawar Valley and surrounding areas, undermining the prevailing economic prosperity. This, in turn, brought about the slow death of a fascinating merger of Indian ideas and Mediterranean execution by the end of the seventh century.

Virtually every Hindu-Buddhist structure in India pays homage to the

Himalayas, but the most sublime Hindu memorial of ancient India was built in the eighth century A.D. some 1,200 miles (2,000 km.) away from its namesake, Mount Kailas. The Cave Temples at Ellora comprise temples and monasteries of the Hindu, Buddhist and Jain faiths. The Kailas Temple, 130 miles (200 km.) north-west of Bombay, is dedicated to Shiva and the shrine was built to represent the Himalayan mountain. Carved out of black volcanic rock, 200,000 tons of igneous stone had to be removed during the construction of an edifice covering twice the area of the Parthenon in Athens and one and a half times as high. Sculptures and reliefs portraying gods, goddesses, animals and monsters from the *Ramayana* together form one of the most magnificent monuments in the world. The impact on seeing the achievement of the unknown sculptors and audacious architects manages, in many ways, to mirror the geological collision that gave rise, literally, to the source of their inspiration

One composition is particularly memorable, showing the demon king, Ravana, imprisoned within the mountain because he attempted to remove it to Ceylon. He is causing earthquakes in his attempt to break free; Parvati clings to Shiva's arm whilst Shiva, imperturbable, keeps control by holding everything beneath his foot. If ever craftsmen's mallets and chisels liberated a concept awaiting their rich imagination, it is in this monolithic shrine quarried on a sloping hillside so far from the source of its inspiration.

Artistic inspiration from the Himalayas, whether in the immediate locality or further abroad, has almost always been expressed through religious themes. Religious persecution too, has played a part, most notably in contributing to the genesis of the Kangra school of miniature painting. Hindu artists trained in the Mogul style were forced to flee from Delhi when the Persian invader, Nadir Shah, plundered the city and massacred the inhabitants in 1739. The painters made for the Punjab Hills, where they gained the Sikh ruler's patronage and established a school specialising in miniatures depicting their patrons as well as the erotic and adventurous life of Krishna. Despite the turbulent times and unruly tribes and chieftains, the art form not only survived but flourished, to be noted in 1820 by the English traveller William Moorcroft, who recorded meeting a ruler, Sansar Chand, employing many artists and possessing a large collection of paintings. Fine and delicate as the lines are in Kangra miniature painting, it is the gossamer lightness of the colours and religious themes idealising feminine beauty which capture the spirit and mood of the time and place in minutest detail.

Tibetan art, like that of Nepal, Bhutan, Sikkim and other parts of the Himalayas, is chiefly expressed in the architecture of palaces, temples, monasteries and stupas—which are locally known as chortens; in sculpture, much of it in bronze; and in the painting of frescoes, mandalas, thangkas and votive banners for temples. The mandala is a mystical circular design symbolising the mind and body of Buddha; the thangka, a rectangular religious painting on cotton that can be rollled up like a scroll.

Palaces and temples form a rich portion of the artistic heritage. The most famous is the Potala Palace (from the Sanskrit, meaning Buddha's Mountain) in Lhasa, residence of the Dalai Lamas from 1650. Its treasures include the stupa of the Fifth Dalai Lama, Ngawang Lobsang

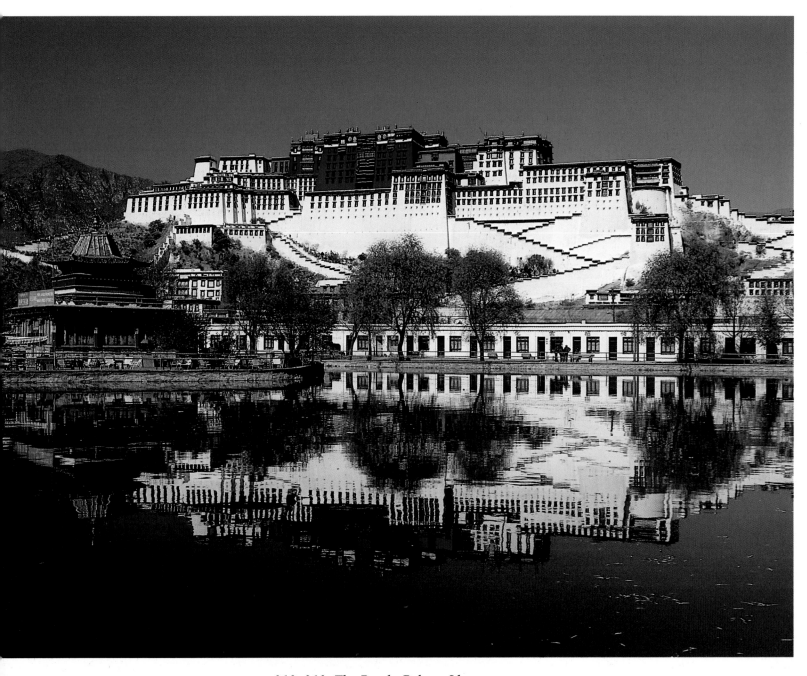

*212, 213. The Potala Palace, Lhasa,
residence of the Dalai Lama until his
exile in India in 1959. Thirteen storeys
high, this vast structure on the Red Hill,
dominating the Tibetan capital, is now a
museum, though still regarded by many
Tibetans as a sacred place. The present
palace was raised on the site of a much
older royal residence in the mid-seventeenth century, in the time of the great
Fifth Dalai Lama, who consolidated the
Tibetan theocracy and the dominance of
the Gelugpa (Yellow Hat) sect.*

214. Monks at the Naqu festival, Tibet. Long, sonorous horns, drums, bells and cymbals are an essential part of all ceremonies and festivities in the Himalayan region.

215. The great 'thangka' at Sera Monastery, near Lhasa, unrolled for display. Huge religious scroll paintings on cloth like this are kept in some of the most important monasteries and shown only once a year. Sera was founded in 1419 by a disciple of Tsongkapa, reformer of Tibetan Buddhism.

*216. In both Tibet and Bhutan, festivals
with traditional dances, colourful masks
and costumes, are important religious
and social occasions. Both laymen and
monks usually participate in the
performances.*

217. Masked dancer at a Buddhist festival at Kumbum Gompa in Amdo province. This is one of the most important monasteries in Tibet as Tsongkapa (1357-1419), founder of the Gelugpa order, was born at Kumbum.

218. A caravan with yaks near Mount Kailas (Tibetan: Kang Rinpoche), southwestern Tibet, an area sacred to Hindus, Buddhists and the devotees of Bon, Tibet's indigenous religion. Yak herding of semi-nomadic type is one of the main means of livelihood in the highest inhabited regions of the Himalayas.

219. Tibetan woman milking a 'dri' (female yak), which gives about a litre a day. Besides providing meat, milk, cheese and butter (also used for lamps), this shaggy, short-legged breed of ox (Bos gruniens), well adapted to the climate, rarified air and rugged terrain, has innumerable other uses. It supplies dung for fuel, hide for leather and hair for weaving, and serves as a pack animal, for riding and even for ploughing.

220. Tiger's Nest (Taktsang) Monastery, perched above a 1,000-metre precipice in the Paro district of western Bhutan, is a sacred place of pilgrimage. It is associated with Guru Rinpoche (Padmasambhava), the 'Second Buddha', who came to Bhutan from India in the eighth century and introduced Tantric Buddhism, which he also took to Tibet.

221. Carved balconies of Lamey Gompa, a beautiful nineteenth-century royal mansion, formerly a royal monastery, in the Bumthang district, central Bhutan.

222. *Rinpung Dzong in Paro, western Bhutan, built in 1645 by the great political and religious leader Ngawang Namgyel, unifier of the country. Dzongs, fortified monasteries, served as the district seats of both religious and civil authority, reflecting the dual system of government that prevailed until the establishment of the monarchy in 1907.*

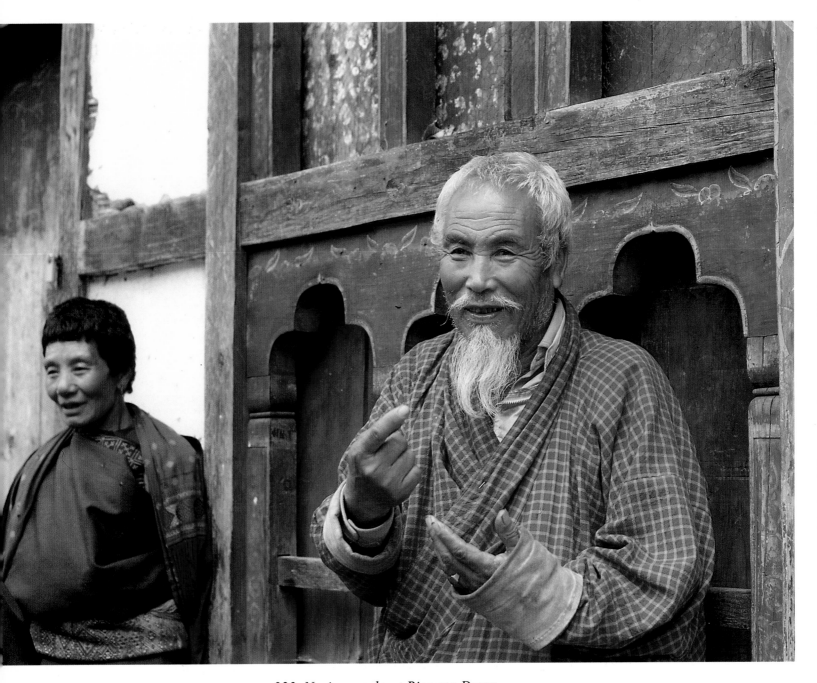

223. Novice monks at Rinpung Dzong, Paro. The Drukpa Kagyudpa school became the dominant monastic order in the first half of the seventeenth century through the influence of Ngawang Namgyel, known as the Shabdrung. The Bhutanese call themselves 'Drukpas' in their own language, Dzongkha.

224. An elderly Bhutanese couple. Average life expectancy in Bhutan has been estimated at only forty-three years, though this is influenced by the high rate of infant mortality.

225. *Pilgrims from Amdo, Tibet, near Lhasa. Buddhists regard the making of a pilgrimage to a holy place as an act of piety. Mahayana Buddhism came to Tibet from India and China in the seventh century. The Tibetan or Lamaist variant lays stress on the oral teaching of a lama (Sanskrit 'guru') for the attainment of spiritual enlightenment.*

226. *Bhutanese girl wearing a colourful necklace of local type.*

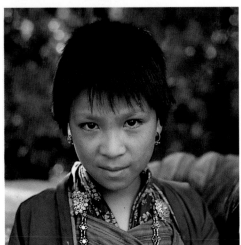

227. Women in Thimphu, capital of
Bhutan (top). Women from all around
come to its famous weekend market, often
to buy woollen yarn, which they weave
with great skill in intricate patterns. The
spinning is still done at home in remoter
regions.

228. Two Tibetan girls. In the
traditionally male-dominated Tibetan
society, women, whatever their class,
were generally regarded as the source of
bad luck and held in subservience.

Gyatso (1617-82), which is covered with 3,700 kilograms of gold and inlaid with gems. Ancient scrolls, illuminated scriptures and many other antiquities and treasures, along with some 200,000 statues, are housed in the 1,000 rooms of this vast, thirteen-storey building.

Mighty fortress-monasteries or dzongs, usually built on almost inaccessible crags or hilltops, are centres of local government as well as religion. Their construction is modelled on the Yumbu Lhakhang Dzong, the most ancient fortress in Tibet, now rebuilt after its destruction in the Cultural Revolution. Tiers of walls, immensely thick and usually filled with mud, rise one above the other, the upper ones being the more recent. The many dzongs of Bhutan, such as the Tongsa Dzong, ancestral seat of the royal family, which contains 20 temples, and the great dzong of the Bhutanese capital, Thimphu, are similar to those of Tibet. The earlier ones had skillfully made wooden roofs, since timber was readily available. Now, corrugated iron or slate is more common.

Wooden architecture, often exquisitely carved and colourfully painted, is a feature of Nepal, where Hindu temples and Buddhist stupas stand side by side. Each aspires to the vertical, soaring towards the heavens: the temples with their series of roofs of decreasing size and the stupas with their tiered structure surmounted by a cupola, above which the eyes of Buddha gaze out on all four sides.

The music of the Himalayas has not travelled well away from the mountains. A westerner accustomed to grandiose oil paintings may respond to the mandala or thangka, but will find the pentatonic folk music awkward on the ear and something of an acquired taste. Religious tradition is expressed in the distinctive, repetitive, throaty chanting of Tibetan mantras, the sonorous bleat of reverberating Lamaistic horns, and the gracious ragas representing moods, such as loneliness, bravery, love, and times of day, such as dawn and evening. Tibetan secular songs are accompanied by the lute or two-stringed fiddle; religious chanting by the long trumpet, drums and cymbals.

Painting, carving, music and religion come together when brilliantly coloured, fantastic masks that are worn for ritual dances and mystery plays performed in temple courtyards on holy days in Tibet, Bhutan, Ladakh and elsewhere in the Himalayas.

Through Western Eyes

Rudyard Kipling, one of the most eminent European writers to be inspired by India, repeatedly expressed the fascination exerted by the hills. Often indicted for writing 'East is East and West is West and never the twain shall meet', the fact is the twain have met in Kipling's compositions and never more than in the Lama of *Kim*. Although Kipling often indicated that the future lay with a mechanical, technologically-regulated world of the western determinist, he could have the Lama solemnly inform Kim, 'Perhaps in a former life it was permitted that I should have rendered thee some service. May be I freed thee from a trap; or, having caught thee on a hook in the days when I was not enlightened, cast thee

229. Young Tibetan woman. In the past, all marriages in Tibet were arranged, and there was no intermarriage between the social classes. Polyandry, once widespread, was much more common among the poor, with several brothers sharing a wife.

back into the River.' It is significant that Kipling often used the swastika on the covers of his books, before the symbol fell into disrepute, and was always alert to the manner in which the way of life in India is thronged with gods.

Another westerner who brought the public a version of the Himalayas they enjoyed was James Hilton (1900-1954), a Cambridge graduate who became a Hollywood scriptwriter and died in California. Though of no great literary merit, his novel *Lost Horizon*, published in 1933, has remained famous because of Shangri-La, a fictitious lamasery dominating a valley in Tibet. The climate, warm by day and cold by night, enables the population of several thousands to live into their second or third century. For example, Father Perrault, the founder, was born in Luxembourg in 1681 and died in 1931 aged two hundred and fifty. He was succeeded by an Englishman, Hugh Conway, who had previously served as His Majesty's Consul in India. It is while this man of destiny, soldier, hero, diplomat, is supervising the evacuation of British refugees that he and others in a plane are hijacked to Shangri-La, where he has been chosen to be installed as High Lama.

Frank Capra directed the film of the book, starring Ronald Colman, which, despite obvious absurdities, was greeted with rapturous praise when it appeared in 1937. Along with Tibetan Art Deco architecture, the lamasery has western central heating, a grand piano —complete with unpublished music by Chopin —and a superb collection of tapestries, ceramics and bronzes. The enormous impact of the film has to be measured against the increasing menace at the time of military developments in Europe and the Far East. Shangri-La's fantasy appealed to the mood of a public wanting peace; the valley of celluloid fiction took on an identity of its own, a fusion of mythmaking from two areas, the Himalayas and Hollywood, where dreams were always in constant supply. President F. D. Roosevelt's country retreat in Maryland was given the name Shangri-La (later it was renamed Camp David). The name was also given by Roosevelt to the 'secret base' (actually aircraft carriers) from which Tokyo was raided in 1942, not the most pacific of undertakings and hardly an appropriate evocation of the tranquil Tibetan lamasery.

The earliest western painted record of the Himalayas is that of Thomas Daniell (1749-1840) and his nephew William (1769-1837), who visited India from 1786 to1794. In spring 1789 they journeyed to Garhwal where they painted landscapes and in a diary reported on the mountains: 'We had a glorious view of snowy ones, or rather regions. The height of them far exceeded any of our expectations... We ascended for about a mile, where the Snowy Mountains made a grand appearance.' The Daniells were also impressed by the hill-men who bartered their produce in the plains, taking back '... salt, copper vessels, and other wares, which they convey not in packs, like our pedestrian traders, but in baskets closely fitted and secured to their backs... In this manner these indefatigable creatures, that seem no larger than ants, compared to the stupendous heights they have to traverse, pursue their laborious journey.'

It was the mountains, however, that really overawed them '... a prodigious range of still more distant mountains, proudly rising above all that we have hitherto considered as most grand and magnificent, and which, clothed in a robe of everlasting snow, seem by their ethereal hue to belong to a region elevated into the clouds... It would be vain to attempt... to convey an idea of those sublime effects, which perhaps even the finest art can but faintly imitate.' Possibly the picturesque temples and sculpture were more saleable subjects or the artists were daunted by the task of imitating such nature; whatever the reason, the enthusiasm of the diary is not reflected in the number of their sketches of the mountains. Nature operates on a gigantic scale in the Himalayas and this book is evidence that the modern photographer can more easily capture the variety of its moods and majesty of its presence.

Rising above the sunlit clarity of the valleys, the grandeur of the Himalayas has always inspired wonder followed by veneration. If the resulting artistic legacy has sometimes seemed modest, it may be because ideas are far more easily conceived, communicated and preserved than fragile works of art, for, paradoxically, those who live in company with the soaring massifs are as spiritually uplifted as they are physically burdened. No matter how sceptical a man may be, the intoxicating scents of conifer resins in the rarefied air, the untrammelled views of sunrise and twilight, the chants of the faithful, cannot but provoke sobering moments of reflection on immortality, and are as vivid as they are an inescapable feature of the abode of snow.

Trimurti, the Hindu trinity of Brahma, Vishnu and Shiva, symbolising the principles of creation, maintenance and destruction, is represented as a body with three heads: Brahma in the centre, Vishnu to the left and Shiva to the right.

283

APPENDIX

STATES OF THE HIMALAYAS

KINGDOM OF BHUTAN
(Drug-yul: Land of the Thunder-dragon)

Capital city: Thimphu
Area: 18,147 sq. mi. (47,000 sq. km.)
Population: 1.4 million
Language: Dzongkha
Religion: Buddhist (70%), Hindu, Muslim

PEOPLE'S REPUBLIC OF CHINA

Autonomous Region of TIBET
(Chinese: Xizang Zizhiqu)

Capital city: Lhasa
Area: 471,700 sq.mi.(1,221,700 sq. km.)
Population: 2.3 million
Language: Tibetan
Religion: Buddhist

REPUBLIC OF INDIA

Federal State of ARUNACHAL PRADESH
(Formerly Northeastern Frontier Agency)

Capital city: Itanagar
Area: 31,439 sq. mi. (81,426 sq. km.)
Population: 865,000
Language: Tibetan-Burmese dialects
Religion: Buddhist, Bon, Animist

Federal State of HIMACHAL PRADESH

Capital city: Simla
Area: 21,490 sq. mi. (55,658 sq. km.)
Population: 5.2 million
Language: Hindi and Pahari
Religion: Hindu

Federal State of JAMMU AND KASHMIR

Capital city: Srinagar (summer), Jammu (winter)
Area: 52,895 sq. mi. (137,000 sq. km.)
Population: 8 million
Language: Urdu, Kashmiri
Religion: Hindu, Muslim

Indian Administrative District of LADAKH

Captial city: Leh
Area (exluding Aksai Chin): 22,517 sq. mi. (58,321 sq. km.)
Population: 150,000
Language: Ladakhi (Tibetan-Burmese)
Religion: Buddhist, Muslim

Federal State of SIKKIM
(Formerly Kingdom of Sikkim)

Capital city: Gangtok
Area: 2,818 sq. mi. (7,299 sq. km.)
Population: 406,000
Language: Lepcha, Bhutia, Nepali, Limboo
Religion: Hindu, Buddhist,

Federal State of UTTAR PRADESH

Captial city: Lucknow
Area: 113,655 sq. mi. (294,366 sq. km.)
Population: 139 million (only one million in mts)
Language: Hindi
Religion: Hindu (82%), Muslim

KINGDOM OF NEPAL

Capital city: Kathmandu
Area: 54,362 sq. mi. (140,798 sq. km.)
Population: 19 million
Language: Nepali, Maithir, Bhojpuri
Religion: Hindu

ISLAMIC REPUBLIC OF PAKISTAN

Province of AZAD JAMMU AND KASHMIR

Capital city: Muzaffarabad
Area: 32,358 sq, mi. (83,806 sq. km.)
Population: 2.5 million
Language: Urdu
Religion: Muslim

INDEX